A Collaborative Approach to Exhibition Making

American Alliance of Museums

The American Alliance of Museums (AAM) is the only organization representing the entire museum field, from art and history museums to science centers and zoos. Since 1906, we have been championing museums through advocacy and providing museum professionals with the resources, knowledge, inspiration, and connections they need to move the field forward.

AAM's mission is to champion equitable and impactful museums by connecting people, fostering learning and community, and nurturing museum excellence.

Books published by AAM further its mission to make standards and best practices for the broad museum community widely available.

A Collaborative Approach to Exhibition Making

Emily Saich and Joey Noelle Scott

ROWMAN & LITTLEFIELD
Lanham • Boulder • New York • London

Rowman & Littlefield
Bloomsbury Publishing Inc, 1385 Broadway, New York, NY 10018, USA
Bloomsbury Publishing Plc, 50 Bedford Square, London, WC1B 3DP, UK
Bloomsbury Publishing Ireland, 29 Earlsfort Terrace, Dublin 2, D02 AY28, Ireland
www.rowman.com

Copyright © 2025 by The Rowman & Littlefield Publishing Group, Inc.

All rights reserved. No part of this publication may be: i) reproduced or transmitted in any form, electronic or mechanical, including photocopying, recording or by means of any information storage or retrieval system without prior permission in writing from the publishers; or ii) used or reproduced in any way for the training, development or operation of artificial intelligence (AI) technologies, including generative AI technologies. The rights holders expressly reserve this publication from the text and data mining exception as per Article 4(3) of the Digital Single Market Directive (EU) 2019/790.

British Library Cataloguing in Publication Information Available

Library of Congress Cataloging-in-Publication Data

Names: Saich, Emily, 1977- author. | Scott, Joey, 1982- author. | American Alliance of Museums.
Title: A collaborative approach to exhibition making / Emily Saich and Joey Scott.
Description: Lanham: Rowman & Littlefield, [2025] | Publication supported by the American Alliance of Museums. | Includes bibliographical references and index.
Summary: "A Collaborative Approach to Exhibition Making offers practical guidance to managing the full life cycle of exhibition projects. Whether you're leading the creation of a new exhibit or engaged in any part of the exhibition making process, you'll find useful and insightful methods to support a collaborative approach"— Provided by publisher.
Identifiers: LCCN 2024055822 (print) | LCCN 2024055823 (ebook) | ISBN 9781538185254 (cloth; alk. paper) | ISBN 9781538185261 (paperback; alk. paper) | ISBN 9781538185278 (electronic)
Subjects: LCSH: Museum exhibits. | Museum exhibits—Planning. | Museums—Management.
Classification: LCC AM151 .S25 2025 (print) | LCC AM151 (ebook) | DDC 069/.5—dc23/eng/20241226
LC record available at https://lccn.loc.gov/2024055822
LC ebook record available at https://lccn.loc.gov/2024055823

For product safety related questions contact productsafety@bloomsbury.com.

♾™ The paper used in this publication meets the minimum requirements of American National Standard for Information Sciences—Permanence of Paper for Printed Library Materials, ANSI/NISO Z39.48-1992.

Contents

Foreword   xi
Acknowledgments   xiii
Introduction   xv

Part 1. Setting Up the Project   **1**

Chapter 1:   **Establishing Process**   3
    Tools and Processes   3
    Exhibition Phases   5
    Documenting Deliverables   8
    Making Your Own Process   10

Chapter 2:   **The Project Brief**   13
    Gathering Information   13
    Sorting Information   15
    Sharing for Review   17

Chapter 3:   **Roles and Responsibilities**   19
    The Project Team   19
    Role Narratives   20
    Coordination Models   23
    Scope Directory   24
    Frameworks for Roles and Responsibilities, Andrea Ledesma   26

Chapter 4:   **The Project Kickoff**   29
    Hosting a Kickoff   29
    Connection Activities   30
    The "Kickoffs" before the "Kickoff," Tiffany Sakato   30

Chapter 5:	**Budgets and Schedules**	33
	Budgets	33
	Contingencies	35
	Schedules	37
	Collaborative Schedule Making	37
	Work Group Plans	39
	Working Side-by-Side with your Architect, Ed Kim	40
Chapter 6:	**Meeting Routines**	43
	Agenda Setting	43
	Status Meetings	43
	Working Meetings	44
	Wall-to-Wall Meetings	44
	Meeting Notes	44

Part 2. Creating the Vision   47

Chapter 7:	**Facilitation**	49
	Facilitating Creativity	49
	Creative Openers	50
	Reading the Room	52
Chapter 8:	**Creative Development**	55
	Basis of Design	55
	Idea Generation	57
	Refining Ideas	60
	Exhibit Summaries	62
	Visual Communication	62
	Design Documentation	64
Chapter 9:	**Prototyping**	71
	Prioritize Prototyping	71
	When and What to Prototype	72
	Testing Materials and Safety	75
	Documenting Results	76
	The Motivation to Prototype, Hagen Tilp	76

Chapter 10:	Feedback	81
	Product Reviews	81
	Excite, Build, Consider	82
	Framing Feedback by Phase	84

Part 3. Finding Alignment — 87

Chapter 11:	Building Rapport to Navigate Change	89
	Humming and Bumming	89
	Shared Values	90
	Project Stops and Starts	91

Chapter 12:	Feasibility	93
	Feasibility Questions	93
	Collective Feasibility	93
	When to Assess Feasibility	95
	Subjectivity and Risk	95

Chapter 13:	Decision-Making	97
	Consensus	97
	Delegation	98
	Up to the Top	98
	Range Voting	98
	SWOT Analysis	99

Chapter 14:	Problem-Solving	103
	Identifying Challenges	103
	Understanding Challenges	104
	Finding Solutions Together	104
	Embracing Challenges to Find Solutions, Cortez Crosby	106

Part 4. Making It Real — 109

Chapter 15:	Engaging Exhibit Contractors	111
	Contractors, Subcontractors, and Vendors	111
	Building Trust	112
	Flexibility from Design to Fabrication	113
	From, Your General Contractor, Shelley Neidernhofer	113

Chapter 16: Developing Scope for Contractors — 115
  Defining Your Needs — 115
  Sample Scopes — 116
  Shop Visits — 118
  Change Orders — 119

Chapter 17: Selecting Contractors — 123
  Request for Qualifications — 123
  Request for Proposals — 125
  Asking Authentic Questions — 127
  Interviewing — 128
  Awarding Contracts — 128

Chapter 18: Communication during Construction — 131
  Owner, Architect, Contractor Meeting — 131
  Daily Site Huddle — 131
  Show and Tell — 132
  A Living Schedule — 132
  Real-Time Drawing Set — 132
  Prioritizing Safety — 133

Chapter 19: On-Site Changes — 135
  Measure Twice, Cut Once — 135
  Anticipate Change — 136
  Schedule, Budget, Quality — 136
  An Approach to Handling Project Changes, Joan Adamczyk — 137

Chapter 20: Completion — 139
  Punchlisting — 139
  Commissioning — 141
  Budget Report — 141
  Schedule Report — 142
  Remediation Report — 142
  Retrospectives — 143

Chapter 21: Celebrating the Work — 145
  Appreciating — 145
  Connecting — 146
  Giving Recognition — 146

Chapter 22:	**Themes and Takeaways**	149
	Thinking Big and Small	149
	Building Resilience	150
	Embracing Curiosity	150
	Valuing People *and* Products	150
	Appreciating Yourself	151

Bibliography	153
Index	159
About the Authors	167

Foreword

It is an honor to be asked to write a forward to Emily and Joey's new book, *A Collaborative Approach to Exhibition Making*. Making museum exhibits has been the core of my professional life for more than 40 years, on the staff of museums and as a consultant, designing, fabricating, and evaluating exhibition work. I have worked *in* historic sites, natural history museums, and children's museums. I have worked *for* botanical gardens, arboretums, science centers, and art museums as well as museums very much like those on whose staff I served. I have also taught graduate museum studies students for almost 20 years as an adjunct professor at the University of the Arts.

Emily and Joey are perfectly placed to put a book like this together—certainly useful to those charged with managing exhibit projects large and small but also for anyone connected to the process. Fundraising professionals, senior administrators, and designers—they all stand to gain from this big to small picture and pragmatic description of the process.

Both authors have served museums for many years in many capacities. Emily managed countless projects for a highly respected exhibit fabrication firm and currently directs major exhibition projects at the Monterey Bay Aquarium. Actively participating on both sides of the table, as client and contractor, gives her a unique perspective on the challenges and insights each can share.

Joey also had invaluable, multidisciplinary experience as a trained teacher and museum educator before moving into exhibition project management. She, more than many exhibit project managers, has a visceral understanding of the heart of this work we do, creating powerful learning opportunities for our visitors.

Both authors understand that a successful exhibition project is more than *on time, on budget*. It's moving an organization's mission forward, meeting its strategic goals, and making experiences that visitors want to return to again and again.

It is also about building enduring teams of both staff and consultant members who feel the same commitment to the mission and spirit of their organization. This book provides a road map to that end. This book also joins a small number of enormously helpful books describing the exhibition-making process and fills an important gap by supporting new and experienced project managers with its straightforward, collaborative, and comprehensive approach. I can imagine dog-eared copies occupying the desks of key players in this strange and wonderful work we do.

Aaron Goldblatt

Acknowledgments

We've been so fortunate to work with brilliant and dedicated colleagues at organizations and exhibition firms across the country. Our incredible contributors and reviewers helped broaden our perspectives and ground our experiences. If you've ever collaborated with us on a project, thank you for your expertise, camaraderie, and inspiration.

Special thanks to Katy Noelle Scott, Rob and Stella Saich, Roux, and Scout.

Introduction

On any given day at any given museum, you might hear children squealing and laughing as they experience a hands-on science phenomenon, see a caregiver's face light up when reading multilingual labels out loud to a young visitor, observe a teen connecting to the natural world through a captivating interactive display, or notice a school group beginning to understand a complex topic related to nature and conservation. These moments that spark joy, connection, *and* understanding are created through informal learning and visitor experiences called exhibitions.[1]

The process of exhibition making can start with a few good ideas and a pile of sticky notes. But it takes many people and many different disciplines to make exhibitions happen.

We find this work incredibly rewarding. And to do it well, you'll need to tune into the nuances and complexity of collaboration. This book is about managing the collaborative process of making exhibitions because the *way* we plan and make has an impact on *what* we plan and make.

We wrote this book for people managing the work of exhibition making and all those involved in the process. While project managers often lead this work, it could also be that content developers and exhibit designers are in the role of managing a project. Or maybe you're a director *and also* your organization's project manager. Perhaps you're just getting into the museum field and joined your first exhibition project as a team member. Or you've been at this for decades and you're looking for new collaborative strategies. If you're involved in leading *or* participating in processes, creative development, schedules, budgets, prototyping, fabrication, or construction of exhibits and exhibitions, this book is for you!

We structured this book in four parts. In Part 1, we focus on setting up the foundation of your project by defining an overall process; developing a project brief; building a team, budget, and schedule; and meeting routines. In Part 2, we share strategies for helping your team generate great ideas and refining those ideas through prototyping, documenting, and generating feedback. In Part 3, we discuss approaches to achieving alignment through assessing feasibility, facilitating decision-making, and problem-solving. In Part 4, we describe how to select and work with contractors to bring your ideas into reality as well as ways to celebrate and close out a project. In some chapters, you'll find a selection of samples and templates to use as a launching point to create your own. Throughout the book, you'll also find seven articles from contributors showcasing best practices and case studies related to exhibition making.

While our book is written in approximate linear progression, creative work rarely moves in a perfectly straight line.[2] In highly collaborative and innovative exhibition work, ideas bounce around and touch many people before they become solid enough to move forward. Doing this work requires flexibility to changing minds, nuance, attention to detail, and a willingness to seek out the expertise of others. Content developers, designers, project managers, fabricators, media producers, writers, editors, translators, scenic artists, curators, mount makers, contractors, and more disciplines with unique expertise and creative minds are all necessary to making exhibitions. This is part of the joy, and complexity, of this work!

The collaborative approach we describe in this book is based on supporting a multidisciplinary team working together, or co-creating, the exhibition ideas *and also* working together to create the process, the budget, and the schedule; how to assess feasibility and choose contractors; and even how to reflect on the success of your project. Exhibits co-created by people from different disciplines, backgrounds, and lived experiences will be more impactful, accessible, buildable, and maintainable. And teams that co-create the process also have a shared understanding, greater clarity, and stronger commitment to *how* they're doing the work together.[3]

Project managers and others on exhibition teams are uniquely placed to support collaboration of creativity and process with flexibility in mind. The tools, processes, and strategies we provide in this book are intended to build your toolbox for managing exhibition projects. Different teams and different projects will all need slightly different approaches to this work. The *Manual of Museum Planning* describes project managers as "delineators, coordinators, communicators, progress monitors, auditors, motivators, and counselors."[4] This book adds a few more: we're also creatives, facilitators, and problem-solvers. Go forth—you've got this! And this book is here to help!

NOTES

1. John H. Falk, *Identity and the Museum Visitor Experience* (Walnut Creek, CA: Left Coast Press, 2009); Nina Simon, *The Participatory Museum* (Museum 2.0, 2010). These texts are foundational resources for understanding the visitor experience through exhibitions, informal learning, and participatory museum practice.
2. Erik Olesund et al., "High Fidelity, Low Resolution," in *Creative Acts for Curious People: How to Think, Create, and Lead in Unconventional Ways* (Ten Speed Press, 2021), 202. "The dominant narrative in our world is that good hard work moves in one direction: forward. But creative work stands apart from other ways of working because it doesn't move in a straight line."

3. Polly McKenna-Cress and Janet A. Kamien, *Creating Exhibitions: Collaboration in the Planning, Development, and Design of Innovative Experiences* (Hoboken, NJ: John Wiley & Sons, Inc., 2013), 19. *"Collaboration . . . is an intrinsic imperative if we intend our museums to be current as well as culturally and socially responsible."*
4. Tom Seiler, "Project Management," in *Manual of Museum Planning: Sustainable Space, Facilities, and Operations*, third edition (Lanham, MD: AltaMira Press, 2012), 541.

Part 1

Setting Up the Project

Getting started on a new exhibition project is exciting. Taking time to set the foundation of a project before diving into creative development will help your team generate and produce ideas that are innovative and grounded in the realities and needs of your organization.[1] This section will dive into processes, routines, and deliverables that create the foundation of your exhibition project. Setting up your project carefully and deliberately *with* your team can yield a variety of benefits:

1. It establishes that everyone is on the same page about the purpose, rationale, scope, budget, and timeline of your project.
2. A set of clear documents can act as an accountability tool to keep teams on track and focused.
3. Referring back to foundational documents throughout a project will inform critical decisions.
4. You'll be able to approach change with more clarity and efficiency.
5. Building the foundation *together* creates energy and excitement right from the start.

Note

1. Robert Garfinkle and Susan Koch, "Project Management and Innovative Exhibitions: A Perfect Pair," in *Are We There Yet? Conversations about Best Practices in Science Exhibition Development* (San Francisco, CA: Exploratorium, 2004), 21. "Exhibits happen in organizations, not in artists' studios. Art can be created without regard to audience or anyone else—an artist can create and then simply see if anyone out there likes it. But exhibit designers live in a world of constraints: There are visitors, stakeholders, clients, board members, and funders, as well as budgets and timelines. Every exhibit resides within some sort of organization, with all the legal, financial, and administrative requirements that even the most institutionally-invisible of projects needs to satisfy."

1

Establishing Process

Leading exhibition making means that you'll create and facilitate processes and provide tools that will support your team's ability to do their best work. A well-used process can be the invisible string that leads to innovation and career-defining projects. Good processes combined with the right balance of tools create space for multiple perspectives, new ideas, diversity of thought, productive disagreement, self-reflection, and camaraderie. Let's start by defining what we mean by tools and processes.

TOOLS AND PROCESSES

We often use the word *tool* to describe a type of document or deliverable that moves a specific part of the process forward. A meeting notes template is a tool, a schedule is a tool, a scoping document is a tool, and a framework for giving feedback is a tool. All of these project management tools support the creation of our end products: graphics, interactives, displays, multimedia, and so on. The schedule, for example, is the guiding tool that connects phases and deliverables together in a logical way, leading to an on-time delivery of your exhibition.

We define a process as a set of agreements about how we work together, which often details who does what, the order it gets done, how we share the work, and when the project moves forward. You'll likely have one overarching process for exhibition making and, within that, several specific processes that roll up under it. Processes need to be carefully managed with the right balance of adherence and flexibility based on your project and your unique team. Have you ever heard someone say that process gets in the way of getting work done? This shows up in phrases like *red tape*, *slowing things down*, and *jumping through hoops*. This could be a sign that you're utilizing tools or processes in a way that's poorly matched to the team or task, which can drain your team's energy. There are things you can do to reframe your approach to tools and processes to overcome this. We've identified four characteristics of a good process that have helped us step back to look at the big picture when it comes to supporting teams and creating innovative exhibitions.

1. **Your process feels like a support system.**

    If you think of your tools and processes as a support system, what would that look like? It should feel reliable, available when you need it most, grounding, and purposeful. And mostly, it should feel foundational and familiar. Yes, we're talking about how things feel for you and your team.[1] You can document every decision and take dictation at every meeting, and still end up redoing work if your team members or decision-makers didn't feel they could speak up, didn't feel heard, didn't feel they could ask questions, didn't feel confident in their authority, or didn't feel they could share their work with others. That's why it's so critical that a process, and the tools you use for creative work, *feel* foundational and familiar. Let's take a closer look at how this might apply to something like a project schedule:
    - **Grounding:** The schedule reflects reality and is achievable.
    - **Purposeful:** The schedule has clear milestones that drive the project forward, and team members take accountability to meet them.
    - **Reliable:** The schedule is updated consistently and based on current information.
    - **Foundational:** The schedule is visible to the entire team and used to set the expectation for what's to come.
    - **Familiar:** The schedule is created using the expertise of team members and shared openly for feedback and coordination.

2. **Your process sets the pace.**

    The idea that processes can slow things down is not wrong, but what if by "processes can slow things down" you really mean "processes can help you be deliberate about pace"? By using a defined process, you can set the pace for different aspects of a project. This might be deliberately making more time for prototyping while setting clear and quick timelines for feedback and approvals. Or setting a more rapid pace at the start of a project so that conceptual work can be shared out early and often for more thoughtful and meaningful feedback and direction. If you have a process that's reliable, clear, and concise, other team members will feel more comfortable waiting for an answer because they know how a decision will be made and how it will be communicated back to them. In an atmosphere where the process doesn't set the pace, everything will feel urgent, and priorities will compete against each other. This can lead to second guessing, redoing good work, exhaustion, and frustration, all of which lead to unintended, and often surprising, setbacks.

3. **Your process encourages collaboration *and* independent work.**
   On highly collaborative projects such as exhibitions, you'll need to find the balance between dedicated time to harness the power of team collaboration and space for people to work individually. Some team members will feel smothered by group work, and they'll need independent time to be creative and productive. Other team members will need to see all the parts and pieces to understand how to do their own work effectively. They'll want continual visibility to what's happening in other areas of the project. A good process can support both of these needs.
4. **Your process makes room for flexibility.**
   Process isn't a stress test, and it shouldn't be laborious. We've read plenty of project management books that frame project managers as rule makers and enforcers, but the best project managers we know are incredibly inspiring and flexible. Make sure your baseline process and tools are documented clearly—this way you don't have to start from scratch every time. Make sure they're also documented *as concisely as possible*—this will afford you more flexibility to adapt to the needs of your specific project team. You shouldn't be expected to come up with a new process for everything evermore, but the reality is that what worked well for one project team may create havoc for another. So, if your process and tools are clear and concise to begin with, you can spend your time facilitating, observing, asking good questions, and customizing it to meet the needs of your team.

EXHIBITION PHASES

A documented exhibition process should start with an overall structure of how the work proceeds through phases. While best practices for developing and designing an exhibition are well documented throughout the exhibitions field,[2] we've found it worthwhile to develop a process specific to your organization and the type of projects you do, with consideration to the staff resources that you have. As a starting point, these are common phases used for exhibition making, and they're the phases we'll use throughout this book:

- **Planning:** In this phase, your main activity is creating a project brief and acquiring approval to launch the project. The planning phase can also include preliminary research and various feasibility assessments[3] or other documents required by your organization, museum leadership team, or funding source in order to launch a project.
- **Concept:** In this phase, you'll create a cohesive content and design vision for the exhibition. This work is often done through a combination of creative brainstorming, research, exploration of precedents, and front-end evaluation. These activities result in the generation of exhibit ideas, exhibit summaries, and visual communication.

- **Schematic:** This is the time for robust prototyping, formative evaluation, and visualizing ideas to make decisions about what works and what will fit within the exhibition. Using this information, you'll produce preliminary cost estimates, feasibility reports, and a schedule to completion. This is a critical phase, at the end of which we recommend a hard stop for review, approval, and alignment.
- **Final design:** Final design is also often referred to as design development.[4] Through further detailing of design drawings, prototyping, feedback, formative evaluation, testing, feasibility results, cost estimating, and scheduling, you should be making final selections on materials, finishes, and dimensions of graphic, exhibit, and media components. If you're required to reduce cost, you'll want to do so at the earliest opportunity so you're only proceeding with final design on work that will move forward into fabrication, production, and construction.
- **Construction documentation:** If your exhibition requires fabrication, general construction and permitting, you'll produce final documentation during this phase for all building, code, and permitting requirements. If you're working directly with contractors or specialty fabricators, they'll often produce construction documentation as shop drawings. This documentation will also be used for either bidding or final pricing from your contractors.
- **Fabrication:** In this phase, you'll engage with specialty fabricators, multimedia producers, graphic contractors, vendors, and others to create unique exhibition components. Fabrication is often completed at specialty shops and shipped to site for installation or, in some cases, produced by in-house staff. This is different from general construction, which typically includes walls, flooring, and infrastructure elements built on-site.
- **Construction and installation:** Work in this phase includes general construction and installation. Specialty exhibit components are often the final items to be installed. Then, final site testing, inspections, punchlisting, and public openings follow.
- **Closeout:** This phase is sometimes short-changed, but it's important to allocate time to thoroughly close out your project. Documentation may include as-built drawings; closeout reports; summative evaluation, including lessons learned; and reflection on the work accomplished to inform planning for your next project.

These phases, while common, aren't entirely linear. There's overlap, and some activities will move ahead of others. For example, long lead time items and media components may need to be ordered ahead of final design in order to meet your construction and installation schedule. We often find that specialty fabrication, such as scenic artistry and mechanical or digital interactives, span multiple phases throughout a project so you can utilize the specific knowledge of exhibit fabricators and media producers to inform final design decisions. In some cases, you'll be required to complete all of your final construction documentation

Phase	Planning	Concept			Schematic		Final Design		Construction Documentation		Construction	Closeout
		50% Concept	75% Concept	100% Concept	75% Schematic	100% Schematic	90% Final Design	100% Final Design	100% CDs	Permitting	Installation	
								Fabrication: Specialty Exhibits & Media				
Selected Deliverables	Project Brief	Big idea, messages, object list	Floor plan, mood boards, exhibit ideas, narrative	Exhibit summaries, renderings, budget, schedule	Elevations, prototypes, feasibility	Exhibit drawings, graphics, prototypes, budget, schedule	Exhibit design package for review feedback	Approved exhibit design package	Package for bidding & construction	Plan checks, permit	Demo, installation, an amazing exhibition!	As-built documentation, O&M manuals, warranties, and retrospectives
Approvals	Official Sign-Off			Official Sign-Off		Official Sign-Off		Official Sign-Off			Punch list	

Figure 1.1 Exhibition-making process overview

for bidding prior to engaging fabricators or builders. In those instances, you'll want to allocate enough time to be able to make some changes to design after they've been contracted. It's also common to step both concept and schematic into progress phases (e.g., 50% concept, 75% concept, and 100% concept) to encourage checkpoints, feedback, iteration, and forward momentum.

In Figure 1.1, you can see the stepped phasing of concept and schematic as well as the overlap of fabrication from the end of schematic through construction documentation. We use this cheat sheet to quickly communicate the overall structure of our process; phases for a typical project; and major deliverables, milestones, and approvals at a glance.

DOCUMENTING DELIVERABLES

Your process document also needs to list the deliverables expected for each phase and who's leading that work. Documenting deliverables isn't just to see which phase has the most work. It's for ownership, accountability, and planning. Deliverables itemized in your process document can then easily be used for progress check-ins, work plan development, prioritizing, scheduling, and leadership updates. During an early iteration of documenting deliverables with one of our teams, we had several pages of deliverables for concept and schematic, and just one deliverable listed for construction—"install it." A construction phase should include items such as build the construction wall, demolition, clean site assessment, staging, wall layout, wall fabrication, electrical and data, lighting installation, painting and wall finishes, flooring installation, exhibit installation, final site testing, punchlisting, cleanup, operations and maintenance manuals, training, and public opening. That's quite a list! In reality, all of the work at each phase can benefit from detailing deliverables. A sample concept phase deliverable list is shown in Table 1.1.

Table 1.1 Concept phase deliverables

Deliverable	*Accountable*	*Collaborators*
Big idea	Content Developer	Exhibit Designer
Content bubble plan	Content Developer	Exhibit Designer
Main messages	Content Developer	Exhibit Designer
Narrative walkthrough	Content Developer	Exhibit Designer
Exhibit summary for each experience	Content Developer	Exhibit Designer, Project Manager

(Continued)

Table 1.1 Concept phase deliverables (*Continued*)

Deliverable	Accountable	Collaborators
Floor plan	Exhibit Designer	Content Developer, Project Manager
Look and feel, materials and color boards	Exhibit Designer	Lead Fabricator, Project Manager
Concept drawings for each experience	Exhibit Designer	Content Developer, Project Manager, Fabricator
Preliminary feasibility for each component	Project Manager	Exhibit Designer, Content Developer, Fabricator
Label hierarchy	Content Developer	Graphic Designer
Graphic types	Graphic Designer	Exhibit Designer, Content Developer
Sample labels	Content Developer	Editor, Translator
Conceptual budget	Project Manager	Exhibit Designer, Graphic Designer, Content Developer, Fabricator
Conceptual schedule	Project Manager	Exhibit Designer, Graphic Designer, Content Developer, Fabricator
Assessment of how we're meeting the project brief goals, considerations, and constraints	Project Manager	Exhibit Designer, Graphic Designer, Content Developer, Fabricator

These are our definitions for the terms we use as column headers in Table 1.1:

- **Deliverable:** A deliverable is an output that documents work and information. Deliverables can include options, recommendations, decisions, and information that guides future work, or they can be the final product. They're often produced in versions, so you may have a first draft of something in the concept phase, a revision in schematic, and a final version in the final design phase. They represent that particular moment in time and are used to either garner feedback from the team or to complete a product.
- **Accountable:** While completing a deliverable may require the work of multiple people, for clarity's sake, one person should be identified as being *accountable* for ensuring that a deliverable is completed. They may also take a lead role in *doing the work* that the deliverable requires. But, more importantly, they're the person most responsible for ensuring it gets

completed, and they have the decision-making authority for *how* it gets completed.
- **Collaborators:** Collaborators are people who are contributing to the deliverable. They support the person who's accountable by contributing ideas, feedback, time, or pieces of work toward the whole. They work in collaboration with, and under the guidance of, the primary person accountable for the work. The deliverable should not be completed without their input, their feedback, or the inclusion of their work and expertise.

MAKING YOUR OWN PROCESS

Creating your own process for making exhibitions as a team will lead to a stronger shared understanding among your team members of how all their work is interconnected. In an ideal world, you'd take a break from projects to get centered on a process that you can all support. Your museum or organization might have a process to build upon, perhaps has never had a process, or has one buried and locked away in a vault. You can start by looking at what you do have and what other similar organizations have, and by thinking about how you can customize it for your project and your team. Even if you create a process and it ends up not working perfectly at first or looking remarkably similar to your old one or every other process diagram out there, it's still a worthwhile endeavor. Defining a process builds a team, and refining a process builds team trust.[5] But the best part of having a documented process is that it allows a team to focus on their work instead of focusing on not knowing what comes next or who does what.

In addition to deliverables, your process should include organizational values about how you work together, collaboration methods, and how you move from one phase to another. An example of how this work could be outlined to align with the concept deliverables is in Textbox 1.1.

Textbox 1.1. Concept phase values, collaboration methods, and phase closeout process

Value we're leaning into during this phase: We will create, design, and produce exhibit experiences to meet our visitors' needs, not our own.

Collaboration Methods

In addition to weekly check-in meetings with the core project team, in this phase we'll engage in a series of design charrettes to generate ideas and in a series of design sprints to refine those ideas. Progress on other deliverables in this phase will be shared regularly at monthly team product reviews with advisers and team collaborators for feedback.

Phase Closeout

1. Deliver the concept package for review and approval to the exhibitions leadership team.
2. Approval process: The concept package is shared with both the steering committee and finance committee for approval to move forward at the end of this phase.

The ultimate goal is to communicate your process in a way that will be easily understood and used by *your* team. Sometimes your projects will be major capital exhibitions, sometimes smaller programmatic exhibits, and everything in between. If you develop a process using the largest and most complex project first, you'll create a more holistic version that can be easily adapted to smaller projects.[6]

NOTES

1. Robert J. Garmston and Bruce M. Wellman, *The Adaptive School: A Sourcebook for Developing Collaborative Groups* (Lanham, MD: Rowman & Littlefield, 2016), 135. "When emotional needs are not addressed in problem solving, tensions persist at a subterranean level, affecting everything else."
2. Maria Piacente, *Manual of Museum Exhibitions* (Lanham, MD: Rowman & Littlefield, 2022), 292-97; Kathleen McLean, *Planning for People in Museum Exhibitions* (Association of Science-Technology Centers, 1993), 48-67; Polly McKenna-Cress and Janet A. Kamien, *Creating Exhibitions: Collaboration in the Planning, Development, and Design of Innovative Experiences* (Hoboken, NJ: John Wiley & Sons, Inc., 2013), 270-300.
3. Barry Lord, Gail Dexter Lord, and Lindsay Martin, *Manual of Museum Planning: Sustainable Space, Facilities, and Operations*, third edition (AltaMira Press, a division of Rowman & Littlefield, 2012), 567; Kathleen McLean, *Planning for People in Museum Exhibitions* (Association of Science-Technology Centers, 1993), 53-54. In addition to assessing feasibility to align exhibit ideas discussed in Chapter 11, McLean discusses the feasibility of overall exhibition ideas in support of the mission, relevance, connectivity, and fundability. Lord, Lord, and Martin discuss feasibility studies of site planning and construction.
4. In the exhibitions field, content is often referred to as "content development," so we find the phrase "final design" to be a clearer description than "design development" for this phase of our work.
5. Andrea Ledesma, notes on iteration of process, July 2, 2024. "When refining a process there is also a need to balance iteration with stability. If the process keeps changing, a team might find it hard to keep up, or reject change itself."

6. Jaap Hoogstraten, emails to Joey Scott, exhibition-making process at the Field Museum, July 2023. "Although this variation [in the different sizes of exhibition projects] makes it difficult to create a process that works for all projects . . . an exhaustive process that provides guidelines for every step of a large project can be scaled down and adapted to organize our efforts for a smaller one. But a process that only addresses the issues that arise when creating smaller projects is of little help when you're tackling much larger ones."

2

The Project Brief

A project brief is a document that sets the guardrails for your project. It includes purpose and logistical details that will guide key decisions along the way.[1] The project brief should hold any information that is critical and relevant to starting and moving down the right path and information you will use through all phases. You may or may not have a project team already identified at this point. Often, project briefs are created for annual or long-term planning or even to submit as project proposals, so this could be well before a team is assigned. We utilize different versions of a project brief for small and discreet projects to the most large, complex, and collaborative projects that we manage, but the process for creating them remains relatively the same each time: gather relevant information, sort that information, and share for review and feedback.

GATHERING INFORMATION

When creating a project brief, gather and source information from as many places as possible. We gather from historical documents, research, data, and prior feasibility studies and evaluations. When combing through documentation that already exists, pull out key points or findings that might have an impact on your potential project. You don't have to ultimately use everything you gather, but more is better at the start.

You'll also want to ask thoughtful and direct questions from as many people as possible. This shouldn't be limited to only who might be on the project team. Cast the net wide for shared buy-in from the start of planning as well as gathering *all* the information you can. This will be useful to confirm the information you already have as well as covering ground in organizations with a history of staff changes, project stops and starts, or uncertain guidance by leadership. Even if many of the requirements for your project have already been documented, collected, and communicated in written form, recognize that not all expertise and knowledge can be found that way. Some people, and some fields, really do lend themselves to verbal knowledge, institutional history and storytelling, or early thoughts and ideas that might not end up in a formal document. Deferring only to what's already in writing biases the information you'll receive and can exclude valuable information that you'll want and need.

You can also confirm key points that you've gathered *and* prompt knowledge and information from other staff or collaborators by hosting inquiry-based meetings. For example, your education team will have knowledge about how people learn, and your evaluation or marketing team may have context on how this project fits into audience needs and expectations or into your brand. Below are some steps and tips for preparing and setting up your inquiry-based meetings.

- **Preparing materials:** Be sure you have access to a large whiteboard or wall to tape or pin things to. Have a stack of sticky notes, index cards, and markers on hand. Before the meeting, write key findings that you already have on the whiteboard.
- **Inviting participants:** Each meeting should be limited to 5 to 10 people. It could help for each group to be at a similar level in the organization so that information is free flowing and low stakes (this will depend on how hierarchical your organization is). Prepare your participants with background information about the project before the meeting if any already exists.
- **Hosting the meeting:** List the categories you want to know more about on the whiteboard. Ask questions related to each of your categories. As people respond, summarize their responses on a sticky note, index card, or digital brainstorming tool and place it under one of the category headings. Some sample questions you might ask include:
    - Why do you think we're doing this project?
    - Are there current issues in this exhibition space we're trying to address?
    - What are the limitations that you already know about?
    - What possibilities for this exhibition have you been thinking about?
    - What would make this project successful?

    As you gather information, ask follow-up questions:

    - Do you agree or disagree with anything already noted?
    - Do you have anything to add?
    - What are we missing?
    - What do you have more questions about?
    - Is this (a specific comment already made) a known constraint/limitation/issue or something to look further into?

- What have you been thinking about but haven't said out loud yet?
- Is there anything already listed that would have an impact on your staff, resources, or planning in other areas?

As you host subsequent meetings, each group will build on the information the previous group provided. This should begin to streamline your questions, you'll begin to see patterns, and it will become obvious where thinking is not aligned. If team members bring up concerns or limitations outside of their role or expertise, it's your responsibility to determine if this needs to be researched further or deferred. You could take that information and turn it into a question on a sticky note and then ask the appropriate team to make the determination if it needs to be addressed or included as part of the project guardrails.

Clarify, but don't change wording whenever possible. If you don't understand something, ask for more information (*Tell me more. What do you mean by that? How would that impact this project?*) or tag it with the person's name to follow up later for more information. Not everything you gather will fit neatly or belong in the project brief at this phase. Sometimes you'll hear ideas and thoughts that are more appropriate for creative brainstorming. Keep this information for creative development and idea generation!

SORTING INFORMATION

Now that you've gathered more information than you need, sorting and organizing this into sections will help you determine what fits and what doesn't. It's also another chance to see where things align or where you have major gaps and contradictions that need to be resolved before you get started on the project. These are the sections we use for an exhibition project brief to set consistent guardrails for most projects:

- **Project description:** Briefly describe the project and any pertinent background information. While this is the first section of our project brief template, we typically draft it last. It's a quick summary or introductory paragraph.
- **Location:** Where is it located? Define the location, ideally with a visual floor plan or map of the area where the project is located along with size and a narrative description of any specific boundaries or landmarks.
- **Purpose and rationale:** Why are you doing this work and whom is it for? This section should clearly identify the purpose, reasons, or issues that are necessitating this project at this moment in time and your intended audience. If the primary purpose of your project, for example, is to create a dedicated art space for pre-K visitors, this will lead you toward certain decisions and not others. Purpose and rationale will guide major decisions, scope, considerations, and constraints throughout the project brief and

the project itself. It will be difficult to assess the importance of information you've gathered if you cannot clearly articulate the purpose and rationale of the project.

- **Project goals:** What will be different when we are done? Project goals should clearly describe what success will look like at the end of this project.
- **Primary scope:** What work is included as part of this project?
- **Additional scope:** Are there other things added to this project for efficiency or convenience but not related to the primary purpose and rationale (e.g., *there are existing plans to replace the lighting track in the gallery space you plan to use for this project. The best time to do this is when the gallery is clear of artwork and furniture*)? In this case, the additional scope may or may not be part of this project budget, but the work certainly needs to be considered within the schedule. This is a great place to keep the concurrent work connected with the primary project for critical coordination.
- **Not in scope:** What is *not included* in the work of this project? Sometimes wish lists will come up when you gather information. If something comes up often enough, it usually has a way of creeping into the project. Determining what is "in scope" versus "not in scope" is an opportunity to be clear from the start so that you spend less time during the project addressing scope creep[2] when it's not necessary.
- **Constraints:** These items are nonnegotiable and must be included or incorporated into the project, or they are clear boundaries for the project. Constraints are one of the keys to productive creative development. You don't want secret constraints, and you don't want any constraints that are not legitimate limits. If constraints are clear and reasonable, your team will be able to focus their energy and attention within the parameters of the project and take creative risks on innovation where it will pay off the most. Over the course of a project, a constraint may change or need to be reconsidered as a project team discovers new information. That's much more reasonable to do if you have clarity in this section to begin with.
- **Considerations:** Considerations are the important thoughts and ideas to consider that are not clear goals, constraints, or scope (e.g., *consider the pros and cons of incorporating a shoes-off infant area for crawlers in the new young learners exhibit. We should investigate our visitors' needs and expectations around an infant area during the concept phase*). Be careful not to repeat items already listed in other sections, and don't include everything and the kitchen sink here. Include only those items that really do need to be considered further, should become part of the creative development process, or need more information than can be assessed in planning. The more clearly and thoughtfully you can describe these considerations, the better, because you'll be asking the project team to spend time and energy resolving them. Set a clear timeline in this section for who, when, and how the considerations will be resolved. We typically state that all considerations

listed in the project brief should be assessed during the concept phase by the project team, with clear recommendations and decisions for each item, before the schematic phase begins. It's also important to be clear that considerations are not just leftover things that a leadership team couldn't decide on. They are the things you really need the expertise within a project team to explore further before making an informed decision.

- **Risks:** What is most likely to jeopardize this project or your organization? Be realistic about risk. Each organization will define risk differently, and it's going to be subjective at this stage. Consider the concerns you've already identified or heard from others. Are there already concerns about the budget, staffing, or issues in the building or gallery space? You want to clearly define here, from a project management perspective, what might prevent this project from being completed on schedule, within budget, or up to quality standards.
- **Operational consequences:** Does this project impact staff, operations, or other projects? If doing this project will require additional staff members or staff will need to drop other priorities or initiatives, this is the place to openly acknowledge these consequences. At times, you might find there are so many operational consequences that it becomes apparent the project is simply not feasible for your organization at this time or without additional time or resources.
- **Budget envelope:** List the budget amount and how you arrived at that number.[3] This will be determined by what you already know about the project and if any previous cost estimates have been done.
- **Schedule:** Overview of the schedule and any critical dates and milestones already established. Include how your schedule was determined, your level of confidence in it, and if there is any flexibility.
- **Team:** What roles do you need for this project, and have team members already been identified for these roles?

SHARING FOR REVIEW

Once you draft the information into a project brief document, it's time for sharing. First, share back with everyone who participated in the information gathering. You should tag people in sections where you still seek clarification and ask for their specific wording or feedback. Ask everyone to review it and provide feedback by a certain date. That sounds easy, but it's most likely the people you gathered information from have the rest of their job to do. This task can get lost in the shuffle, especially if it's a lengthy document. Recognizing that, we typically offer three ways to provide feedback at this stage:

1. Review and comment within the document.
2. Attend a meeting in person or virtually to talk through the feedback.
3. Attend a walk-through of the document at the proposed project site.

The third option is important. Offering an option to review the document at the proposed project site also provides an opportunity to further clarify any physical aspects, confirm the location is understood, and take photos for inclusion as supporting documentation.

You should now be able to clarify, edit, and consolidate the draft project brief based on the feedback you gathered. Then, share the document again to get final feedback before it goes to your leadership team or a steering committee for approval to proceed.

NOTES

1. Project Management Institute, *A Guide to the Project Management Body of Knowledge (PMBOK® Guide)*, 72; Denise Canty, *Agile for Project Managers* (New York: CRC Press, 2015), 80–82; Martha Morris, *Managing People and Projects in Museums: Strategies That Work* (Rowman & Littlefield, 2017), 79–94. Project initiation documents, such as project briefs, are also called project charters. In classic project management, project charters include purpose, requirements, risks, schedule, and budget. We prefer to use the project brief format to account for more narrative and broad scope and constraints as they relate to larger organizations and museum exhibition projects. Charters can be used for discreet projects that are more concise in nature.
2. Adrian Abramovici, "Controlling Scope Creep," PM Network, 2000, accessed July 12, 2024, https://www.pmi.org/learning/library/controlling-scope-creep-4614. Scope creep is the slow but consistent growth of your original scope. It will often add both time and expense to the project as a whole and should be avoided to ensure project delivery within the set schedule and budget.
3. Kristin Hill, Katherine Copeland, and Christian Pikel, eds., *Target Value Delivery: Practitioner Guidebook to Implementation* (Arlington, VA: Lean Construction Institute, 2016), 162. Lean construction calls this initial budget "Expected Cost" and describes it as *"Expected Cost is the amount the owner is willing to spend for the total project."*

3

Roles and Responsibilities

Roles and responsibilities often overlap on complex and creative projects. When you're covering new ground, things might not be as clear as something that is more programmatic or operational in nature. In this case, you can define roles and responsibilities with respect to creating a shared understanding of each primary *role* rather than clear-cut boundaries between the *tasks* people do. Roles and responsibilities should be something you create *with* your collaborators rather than *for* your collaborators.[1] Doing so will serve to increase the collective intelligence of your team and allow people to work more effectively together.[2]

THE PROJECT TEAM

Early in your project, you'll need to understand who is on your team.[3] Team members might already be assigned by your organization, but hopefully it's something you have input on based on the project needs outlined in the project brief. There is a sweet spot where team members and team size match perfectly and everyone feels purposeful and fulfilled. But often you'll find you're missing a role or two. Those roles may need to be filled with outside consultants, advisers, or contractors.

If you're working on a project that's particularly exciting or impactful, you may find that more staff want to be involved than can be productive. This can be resolved by establishing clear lines for communication, creating processes for how you gather input and feedback, or by using a responsibility matrix or other tool. Sometimes it simply cannot be solved, and you'll have a few extra people in the room. Over time and with the building of trust, this might also resolve on its own. In some organizations, you'll also run into the issue of many people wanting to be consulted and offering opinions, but very few available to do the work. This is problematic and can also be addressed through finding balance between giving people the information they need to succeed and being clear about input the team needs to make progress.

On exhibition projects, we tend to define four major categories of team members:

1. **Leadership team:** These people will be your primary advisers who provide feedback and approval throughout the project and who should be consulted on high-risk items.
2. **Project team:** Primary working team members who lead each area, do the work, and can communicate and carry information to extended team members, also sometimes referred to as a core team or working team.
3. **Extended project team:** Team members who are brought in for specific tasks or phases or who represent one specialized aspect on the project but are not necessarily full-time on this project beginning to end.
4. **Consultants, advisers, and contractors:** These are resources outside of your organization required to complete your project. They could be writers and editors, exhibit designers, architects, safety consultants, audience advisers, media producers, specialty fabricators, and on and on. While they may play key roles on your project, your in-house team is responsible for defining their work, managing their work, final decision-making, and long-term maintainability of what they produce for you.

Once you've established your team members, you should work together to clearly define their roles for this project. We're not necessarily talking about job descriptions when we define roles on a project. While they are informed by someone's job description, these are specific roles that a team member will play on a specific project or part of a project. The method you choose will depend on how your team works together to begin with and if you have well-established roles, procedures, and working methods already in place or not. We use a combination of role narratives, coordination models, and scope directories depending on the phase we're in and the clarity we need.

ROLE NARRATIVES

We begin the process of building narratives by asking each team member to write down on a large sticky note one sentence that best describes their primary role on *this project*. We don't discuss these as a group quite yet, but we collect them and review to see if they generally match our understanding of their role. If everything matches, great! You can document this, share it with the team, and your work is done. The wonderful thing about this method is that team members are using their own words. Similar to how asking staff to develop their own goals impacts their sense of ownership,[4] we've observed that people seem to take more ownership over things they say about their own roles on a project. We find role narratives most helpful during planning, right before or after a project kickoff, or during early concept.

A few other things might happen through this process:

- You may find there are significant gaps in the work people claim and the work that needs to be done. This could mean you need to discuss expectations with some individuals, seek clarity from your leadership team on expectations, or supplement with contractors. It could also mean that a few sentences just don't cover it all, and you'll need to use one of the more detailed tools below to further understand what's really missing.
- Sometimes roles will conflict or overlap too much with each other, especially as they relate to authority in decision-making. This is a problem that can be resolved better at early stages, and it will save you much headache later. If there is enough trust already built within your team, you could ask the folks with overlapping roles to work together to define this more clearly in relation to each other. If needed, you could ask for support from their managers.
- Sometimes the words people use to describe themselves don't fit predefined structure or hierarchy within your organization. For example, someone with a lead role describes themselves as "contributing to," and someone with a supporting role describes themselves as "leading." Reach out to them individually to find out why your perceptions don't align.

After you've addressed any discrepancies, send the whole document back to the team and ask for confirmation or clarification. Textbox 3.1 shows an example of role narratives for a mid-sized project. This gives everyone a chance to see the big picture and to see their own role in relation to others.

Textbox 3.1. Role narrative samples

Team Roles and Responsibilities

Director or Head of Exhibitions

Primary responsibility: Provides overall vision to ensure the project meets goals and standards for exhibitions. Ensures the project team has the resources (time, budget, staff) to be successful. Provides final decision-making when required.

Project Manager

Primary responsibility: Provides project oversight from concept through construction, including creating and managing the budget and schedule and documenting feasibility and decision-making. Facilitates processes for collaborative work. Plans and manages contracting and major construction activities with architects and contractors.

Content Developer or Curator

Primary responsibility: Provides overall conceptual development, content research, and decisions about exhibit messaging and visitor experience goals. Writes exhibit labels. Oversees evaluation planning. Provides input on schedule and budget.

Exhibit Designer

Primary responsibility: Provides overall design vision and creates design solutions. Creates two-dimensional and three-dimensional visual design documents from concept through construction, and tracks design decisions. Working with the project manager, coordinates with the work of architects, specialty fabricators, and general construction contractors. Provides input on schedule and budget. Supports documentation for permitting.

Multimedia Designer

Primary responsibility: Designs and produces media and multimedia components and oversees associated contracting.

Exhibit Fabricator

Primary responsibility: Contributes to design of mechanical interactives. Contributes to feasibility assessments. Provides overall exhibit prototyping and exhibit fabrication.

Education Representative

Primary responsibility: Provides educational resources and expertise on informal learning. Assists in determining if designed ideas are developmentally appropriate for the intended audience.

Guest Experience/Visitor Services Representative

Primary responsibility: Provides expertise on the daily visitor experience, visitor and staff needs, and guest navigation.

COORDINATION MODELS

If you're making physical things as part of your project, such as cabinetry, casework, vitrines, a mechanical interactive, digital interactive with monitors, loose parts, a water play table, seating, walls, whatever it may be—a visual representation of responsibilities can go a long way. It's also helpful to establish overlap where on-site coordination is needed. This can be especially helpful both in early design phases *and* later phases, such as construction and installation. In our case, we sketch this by work groups rather than individuals. Overlaps are very easy to see because you'll see two things touch each other. For example, if one work group is responsible for monitors and another is responsible for walls, they will clearly need to communicate and coordinate the wall structure and blocking for monitor placement and who/how/when the monitors get installed.

A coordination model can be produced as a set of detailed drawings and elevations, but it can also start with a simple hand sketch. Shown in Figures 3.1 and 3.2 are two different examples of coordination models: one using an elevation and another using a cross-section. Choose the type of model that best communicates coordination with your team and create your own visual with elements that will appear in your project or exhibition.

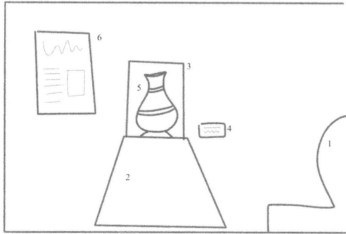

Figure 3.1 Coordination model example—elevation

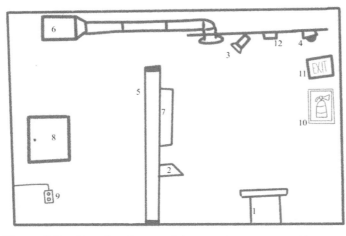

Figure 3.2 Coordination model example—cross-section

SCOPE DIRECTORY

Creating a scope directory can be very useful as you get into schematic through final design phases when multiple people are responsible to create one product. If you're working on a project large enough for multiple project managers or designers (both in-house and contracted), this will help you clearly establish scoping between each project manager. In this tool, as shown in Table 3.1, there is still one person accountable, and this person ensures the work is planned and completed accurately and on time. People listed as accountable are most often project managers or leads in their respective discipline.

In addition to accountable, this scope directory includes three columns of responsibility:

1. Responsible for design and documentation
2. Responsible for accuracy and quality control
3. Responsible for fabrication or construction

Roles listed in the responsibility columns are often staff members, contractors, or vendors. The final column is a gathering place for other notes, links, or nuances that need to be added. At the point where a scope directory document becomes most useful, much of the consulting and informing have already happened, and we are focused on reviewing for accuracy and completion.

Table 3.1 Scope directory sample

Project name:
Date:
Compiled by:

Areas of work	Accountable	Responsible for design and documentation	Responsible for accuracy and quality control	Responsible for fabrication or construction	Other notes
Furniture, casework, vitrines					
Multimedia elements					
Mechanical interactives					
Interpretive graphic panels					
Electrical, mechanical, plumbing systems					

FRAMEWORKS FOR ROLES AND RESPONSIBILITIES
by Andrea Ledesma

Delegating work or sharing project updates can sometimes feel like an Abbott and Costello bit. Instead of asking "who's on first?" we ask "who's responsible for this?"

As senior manager for strategy and operations, I implement and iterate workflows and standards for large collaborative teams. Clear roles and responsibilities are critical. We collaborate extensively across the organization. A consistent method for organizing teams, recognizing their expertise, and documenting their involvement in the project is crucial to its success.

We've tried a handful of frameworks. There's RACI: responsible, accountable, consulted, and informed. Given its popularity and simplicity, this was easy to socialize, but the difference between responsible and accountable wasn't always clear.

We moved on to MOCHA: manager, owner, consulted, helper, and approver. Many liked helper, as many hands move work forward. However, the manager, owner, and approver roles created some unnecessary complexity.

We even attempted to create our own framework. For example, we included consulted, helper, and informed to more clearly signal to collaborators who would:

- Offer expertise and insight (subject matter experts)
- Do/complete the work (task assignees, team members)
- Keep an eye on project status and its potential impact (leadership)

The custom framework remains a work in progress as we pursue a combination of roles that serve our team and are easy to apply and adapt.

Regardless of the acronym, here's what we know works well:

- **Document and socialize the role framework.** The best tool is the one that people use. As we iterate on processes, we draft playbooks or templates to onboard and update teams to new/updated processes.
- **Establish roles at the start.** Team members should know their roles and goals early and often. Walk the team through the document when you kick off a project and find ways to keep this information top of mind.

Remember that these are living documents. Roles and responsibilities may change over time. That's okay! Reconvene around major milestones or the end of a phase to review roles and edit them as needed.

NOTES

1. Anita Williams Woolley et al., "Bringing in the Experts: How Team Composition and Collaborative Planning Jointly Shape Analytic Effectiveness," *Small Group Research* 39, no. 3 (June 1, 2008): 352-71, https://doi.org/10.1177/1046496408317792.
2. Anita Williams Woolley et al., "Evidence for a Collective Intelligence Factor in the Performance of Human Groups," *Science* 330, no. 6004 (October 29, 2010): 686-88, https://doi.org/10.1126/science.1193147.
3. Sarah J. Chicone and Richard A. Kissel, *Dinosaurs and Dioramas: Creating Natural History Exhibitions* (Walnut Creek, CA: Left Coast Press, 2014), 37-48; "25th Anniversary Issue," *Exhibition: A Journal of Exhibition Theory & Practice for Museum Professionals* 25, no. 1 (season-01 2006): 71-77, https://www.aam-us.org/wp-content/uploads/2024/04/spring2006NAME__FULL.pdf. *Dinosaurs and Dioramas* includes brief descriptions of common roles within museum exhibition projects, such as project manager, developer, content specialist/curator, designer, registrar, educator, evaluator, fabricator, media designer, visitor services manager, and marketing specialist. The spring 2006 edition of *Exhibition Journal* (formerly *Exhibitionist*) includes articles describing four common roles within exhibition making: *"A Project Manager Is . . ."* by Jennifer Bine, *"An Exhibit Developer Is . . ."* by Penny Jennings, *"An Exhibit Designer Is . . ."* by James Sims, and *"What's a Museum Evaluator?"* by Jeff Hayward.
4. Sabeeh Pervaiz, Guohao Li, and Qi He, "The Mechanism of Goal-Setting Participation's Impact on Employees' Proactive Behavior, Moderated Mediation Role of Power Distance," *PLoS One* 16, no. 12 (December 15, 2021): e0260625, https://doi.org/10.1371/journal.pone.0260625.

4

The Project Kickoff

Now that you have guiding and foundational documents and a team put together, it's time to kick off your project. A great project kickoff meeting can develop commitment, excitement, and, above all, a deep understanding of how a team will work together. Bringing the full project team together, including those who might have a smaller part to play, is essential here. Without it, the early stages of a project can get unwieldy with people quickly moving in different directions. Just about every time we've tried to skip a project kickoff meeting because "this project is too small" or "everyone already knows how to do this" or "it's just like the last project," we find we have to stop and redirect later to create the shared project understanding we're continually seeking.

HOSTING A KICKOFF

The impact of a project kickoff is long-lasting, so it's worth the time to plan in advance, set up a comfortable space, and prepare materials. We recommend holding the meeting in a conference or collaboration room that will be a home base for your project. A project kickoff might be under an hour or up to a full day depending on the size and complexity of your team.

A project kickoff should include time for the team to connect and to discuss three main questions:

1. **What is this project?** Share the approved project brief, with an emphasis on scope, schedule, and budget, along with any creative intent already established. Include a discussion of what success looks like for this project and this team.
2. **Who is on the team?** Discussion of roles and responsibilities, understanding each other's expertise and what each person brings to this project. This is why your invitee list should include people from across your

organization who will work on this project. It might also include contractors, consultants, advisers, or community liaisons.
3. **How will we work together?** Discussion of the tools, strategies, and routines that the team will use, including conversations about decision-making and software programs.

CONNECTION ACTIVITIES

A good kickoff meeting is usually an interactive meeting. Here are three activities to consider trying out. We don't recommend doing all these activities; instead, choose one that makes the most sense for your team.

1. **Your successful project:** This is a simple activity that asks participants to write down or say out loud how they will know if the project is successful. Ask them to think about the project from their expertise or point of view. Responses may range from "fewer calls to fix things" from your maintenance team, to creating "a space that feels welcoming to everyone and allows for people to make personal connections." Group alike things, discuss, and keep this posted or documented in a shared space.
2. **Immersion activity:** Starting off the project with an immersive, shared experience can form a strong bond between team members and develop excitement for the topic. For example, on a project about wetlands, the project team started the kickoff with an early morning guided bird-watching tour with a local expert.
3. **Retrospective review:** If you did a retrospective or reflection session at the end of your last project, this is a great time to refer to the lessons learned and recommendations made by your team about process and collaboration. Review those recommendations and discuss how you will implement them.

At the end of the kickoff, draft the meeting notes, including any participant-generated notes from the connection activities. These can be helpful if you need to refer back to them later in the project.

THE "KICKOFFS" BEFORE THE "KICKOFF"
by Tiffany Sakato

In football, a kickoff doesn't actually begin at the start of the field but, rather, at the center of it. I find this an apt visual when thinking about organizing a project kickoff for a new exhibition. Pulling off an exhibition is a highly complex endeavor, no matter how small your institution is or how seasoned your colleagues are in working with each other. It is always a big opportunity for everyone involved. It is a process that is loaded with significant situational and psychological uncertainty and whose successful conversion from dreams to reality depends on the participation of many different people. That is why investing in lowercase *k* kickoffs leading up to the formal project kickoff can be immensely helpful. It can ensure that the eventual action at the center of the field moves smoothly in the right direction.

In these pre-kickoff kickoffs, if you will, the project brief is a key reference document. A lot of effort was likely put into this document. As the project manager receiving it, you should know it like the back of your hand. Scrutinize it and take initiative to meet with the original drafters of the brief to ask any clarifying and "dumb" questions and get an early sense of thoughts, feelings, and preferences that may not be so evident on the page. Should there be conflicting views or assumptions among the original drafters, this is a great indicator that more work needs to be done at the project's sponsorship or leadership level. A revised brief may need to be issued, which is fine. Better to have it happen at this stage of the process than have discrepancies and awkward debate break out in front of a broader audience at the project kickoff.

Once you feel confident enough in the stability of the project brief, then it's time to start developing your "insiders" group. These are the folks who are likely listed in the project brief as core team members and extended team members and will be at the project kickoff. Also, there will always be other key people who may not have a formal job on the project but whose attitude, support, connections, and position within the institution are critical. Work to identify these people early and start getting to know them.

Before the project kickoff gets booked, try to meet with your insiders one-on-one wherever *they* work. If it's out on the public floor, meet in a quieter area on the floor and chat. If it's on the rooftop, meet them there and remark upon their awesome view! These "home visits" accomplish many things. They make it convenient for the person you're trying to meet with; you're literally bringing the meeting to them. By seeking them out face-to-face, you're indicating interest in and respect for the work they do. Plus, the visit can stimulate humanizing conversations beyond the project at hand. Relationship and empathy building are *everything* at this stage of the process. You're also gaining an overarching appreciation for the range of people and expertise this project will ultimately draw on. There is an incredible breadth of working conditions and styles your project members operate under; keep that in your mind as you plot the collaborative work to come.

In these one-on-ones, the goal for you, the project manager, is to develop rapport and demonstrate your professional competency as well as respect for this team member. Use these tailored, individual kickoffs to:

- Introduce yourself and express your excitement to be working with the person.
- Recap what's going on with the project and inform the person that there will be a project kickoff coming up "soon." This is a chance to verify if a date, time, and location you're thinking of is suitable or makes sense to adjust.
- Clarify who is coming to the project kickoff, who is not, and in what capacity.
- Make sure the person has a copy of the project brief and go through it together.
- Recap what you know about the project and check for common understanding.
- Detect how deep the person's exposure to the project goes and help fill in gaps and clear up outdated information or assumptions they may still be carrying since the project brief was approved.
- Ask what the person thinks is important to be sure to cover at the project kickoff.
- Ask what tools, systems, and work schedules this person and/or their team operates on. Knowing this will help shape the norms of the cross-functional project team.
- Confirm that this person will attend the project kickoff. This sounds very basic, but getting verbal commitment is powerful at this stage.

Taking the time to meet one-on-one telegraphs the significance of the imminent project kickoff and the person's relevance. This effort builds their buy-in. Use the occasion to state that the project kickoff will start and end on time and will follow an agenda, and that their attendance is critical. They are an insider. Take the time to explain what will happen after the project kickoff (e.g., slides and minutes from the meeting will be shared, core team will start meeting weekly, a research trip is in the works). Previewing this plan of action can help the person feel like the project is really happening and that they are getting an advance peek into the initiation period. Ask, "How does this sound to you?" and then listen. Often, your insider will offer advice or hint at a valid concern that you can address at the project kickoff without putting them on the spot.

Preparing for these kickoffs before the project kickoff does take time and effort. But the upshots for doing so will only strengthen your understanding of the project you're leading and the connections you have to the project members and other collaborators. By putting in the miles up front, the goal is to convene a project kickoff where there are many meeting insiders.

5

Budgets and Schedules

Budget and schedule might be the top two items people think of in regard to project management. While they are definitely high on the list of primary responsibilities for project managers, we find they are better created as *team products*. That said, it's up to the project manager to engage the team in their creation. The way you create and manage the budget and schedule can either reduce urgent emergencies at crucial moments or lead to misalignment, mistakes, and backtracking. The project manager should provide consistent and clear communication about budget and schedule to team members throughout the span of a project. These tools have a big impact on your project, and you'll want to carefully manage them in a way that supports your team's ability to do their best work.

BUDGETS

If you're managing a project, you'll be expected to deliver a project budget at each phase of work. Your budget should get more detailed, descriptive, and accurate with each decision and phase. There are few things more discouraging than cutting innovative ideas because of budget surprises after you engage contractors or specialty fabricators. Because of this, we recommend treating the budget as iteratively as your development and design process. When you're in concept, create a conceptual budget. When you're in schematic, create a schematic estimate. And so on. You'll also likely need to communicate this to a leadership team, a project sponsor,[1] or a finance committee for approval, so it helps to establish shared terminology you can all support. Below are budget descriptions that align with common exhibition-making phases.

- **Budget envelope:** This is often referred to as a target budget or allocated budget created during the planning phase. Your initial budget envelope might be based on square foot estimates from your last project, perhaps you received a specific donation for the exhibition, or there is a capital project plan with a preset budget. Whatever the case, be clear about the budget envelope that you have to start with. If you don't have any of these parameters, use historical knowledge to come up with a budget range for the project and be transparent about what this is based on. This budget envelope is the furthest from the end product, and so it's likely to be the least informed by what you plan to do (because you haven't come up with all the great exhibition ideas yet). If you don't have operational budgets that cover maintenance and technology upgrades after the exhibition is open, consider including them in your budget envelope from the start.

- **Conceptual budget:** During the concept design of your project, you should be creating a conceptual budget. This is a collaborative effort and should include the core project team, consultants, specialty fabricators with specific expertise, and perhaps even a professional estimator. The goal of the conceptual budget is to begin identifying the categories of cost you'll need to account for in this particular project for both design and construction. At this phase, it's most important to identify the categories and key line items. Include any budgets, preliminary cost estimates, or allowances for each category as well as a healthy contingency.
- **Schematic estimate:** At this phase, you should be able to identify specific line items and associated costs for the project. The more detail, the better, and every line item should have a dollar amount associated with it. You should also identify how you arrived at the estimate for each line item. Was it estimated by a fabricator or trade partner, by researching parts and material costs from a vendor, by your internal team, or by an estimating consultant, or is it still just an allocation or educated guess? The important thing at this phase of the project is that none of your line items should be blank. An example of a line-item detail for a schematic phase estimate is in Table 5.1.
- **Final cost estimate:** Final pricing and cost estimates should be provided by contractors, fabricators, vendors, multimedia producers, and trade partners based on detailed drawings with material and part specifications. You may end up contracting one large firm with many subcontractors. In this case, you'll want to see all subcontractor pricing as well as prime contractor markups to fully understand what goes into your final cost estimate. Exhibition projects often have many parts and pieces. Even if you have one prime contractor, you'll likely also have internal project costs that you'll need to account for or specialty contractors that you prefer to manage directly. It's important to look at all of these parts as a whole to understand your final cost estimate.
- **Tracking:** Once you have confirmed pricing, it's best practice to track the actual money spent at each phase on each major contract. This will help

Table 5.1 Schematic estimate sample

Component	Estimate	Type
Title wall graphic	$1,500	Historical cost
Redwood tree model	$85,000	Fabricator estimate
Interpretive graphics	$5,000	Based on square footage
Translation	$5,000	Historical cost
Multimedia interactive	$30,000	Contractor estimate
Tree trunk seating cushions	$2,000	Price from vendor
Selection of books and props	$1,000	Allocation
Demolition and site prep	$15,000	Contractor estimate
Wall finishes	$5,500	In-house paint team estimate
Safety consultant	$2,000	Fixed fee
Subtotal	**$152,000**	
Contingency	$30,400	20% of subtotal
Total	**$182,400**	

to avoid last-minute budget surprises. It will also support sound decision-making on changes and use of your contingency, and inform budget envelopes on future projects. At each phase, be transparent with your team. If you have designers, collaborators, and other creative decision-makers on your team, they should be in lockstep with you on budget. Your leadership team will also need transparency and communication from you on money spent and what your projected cost to completion[2] will be. A budget variance sample is in Table 5.2. This will help you track actuals and compare them with your budget allotments.

Table 5.2 Budget variance sample

Item description	Estimated cost	Actual cost
Translation services	$5,000	$4,550
Tree trunk seating cushions	$2,000	$2,025
Selection of books and props	$1,000	$850
Total	**$8,000**	**$7,425**

CONTINGENCIES

Including a contingency in your budget is one aspect of risk management.[3] A contingency accounts for something you have not yet identified. Exhibitions are full of new, innovative, and novel ideas (as they should be). So you're sure to have something unaccounted for, and holding a contingency is a responsible way to manage this risk. Contingency should be applied as a percentage throughout your project, starting with the budget envelope and conceptual budget phases. As you gain more information about your project and more specific details, your contingency percentage will decrease as that money becomes accounted for in your line items, as shown in Table 5.3. We recommend the project manager hold the authority to manage and release contingency throughout the project. If you manage this correctly, you'll use all of your contingency by the end of the project or maybe even have a little left over, but you won't go over.

Often, we find that people outside of planning and project management see contingency as money you won't need to use, and they'll want to remove it from the project at the start. When that happens, you'll have nothing to account for material escalation, incremental delays or issues on-site, or even a change request by your own team.

There are typically three main types of contingencies that are helpful to understand:

1. **Design contingency:** This will account for unknowns or changes during design and will allow you and your architects or designers to explore options and approaches with some flexibility in cost. It will also allow you to ask for changes in the design phases without significant impact to the project and will cover design changes that occur from code requirements discovered during design.
2. **Construction contingency:** This will account for contractor-directed schedule acceleration, overtime work to make up for lost time related to contractor delays and scope gap between subcontractors, and changes in materials and construction as well as omissions, errors, and on-site changes. This can include material escalation, which is the change in material and labor cost over time if your project is more than one year out from construction.
3. **Owner contingency:** This is a contingency held by you (the owner) for changes that you request, delays caused by the owner, unforeseen conditions, or the selection of additional or alternate solutions along the way.

Table 5.3 Types of contingencies

Type of contingency	Held by	Held at Concept	Held at Schematic	Held at Construction
Design	Architects or designers	15%	10%	5%
Construction	Contractor	10%	10%	10%
Owner	Museum	20%	15%	10%

The owner is often required to release contingency funds, so your contractor or fabricator should not be pulling from a contingency without providing you an estimate and allowing for your approval before proceeding. Any unused design or construction contingency should eventually convert back to an owner contingency. In some contracts, owners and contractors split the unused contingency as an effort to encourage choosing the better value solutions.

SCHEDULES

Ask a dozen project managers what makes a good project schedule, and the top answer you'll get is buffer time. Making sure your project schedule has time for the (expected) unexpected is one key to success. While that might be true, in our experience the best project schedules are created *together* with a realistic assessment of what it takes to do the work from the people actually doing the work. We support an approach that values the experience of individuals and asks them to contribute to the schedule in a meaningful way.

The schedule-making process we'll describe is based on pull planning,[4] which is sometimes used in construction. We've had success using it on all types and sizes of projects. A key feature is that you work backward from a milestone date, which is different from classic critical-path[5] scheduling, where you look at the list of activities that must be done in order from beginning to end. We find that more classic processes leave those whose work happens at the end of a project in a crunch. This collaborative process, on the other hand, encourages hearing directly from those responsible for doing the work, starting from a critical date and then *working backward*. This is where the most empathy and understanding happen. It's where the real talk comes out. It's where we start to create a schedule *together* with shared ownership and shared responsibility.

COLLABORATIVE SCHEDULE MAKING

The following outlines our process for collaborative schedule making for one phase of an exhibition development and design process.

1. Gather teams or one primary representative from each work group together around a large-format calendar that includes the end date for the phase you're scheduling.
2. Review the date for phase completion and the primary goals you're trying to achieve by this date. We encourage open discussion so that everyone understands the reasoning behind this date and how moveable (or not) it is.
3. Each work group uses one sticky note for each major deliverable or activity they will complete during this phase. We like to give each work group

different color sticky notes to help visualize who is taking the lead on each item. See an example in Figure 5.1.
4. On each sticky note, the work group identifies how long it will take to complete the deliverable, who is responsible for delivering it, what it requires (a dependency), and what it informs (what comes next).
5. Begin by asking what the last thing is that needs to be delivered in this phase. Add that sticky note to the calendar, and work your way backward based on the dependencies identified, rotating through different work groups until all the sticky notes have been added to the calendar.
6. Reflect with your team during this process and resolve any questions that arise. What did they learn about other people's work? How does this impact their work? Are there any major conflicts or nonnegotiables that came up? Are there any surprises that need to be resolved?
7. Use the calendar and sticky notes to create work plans and an overall project schedule.
8. Post physical calendars in a shared space and keep them updated as a digital tool so that everyone has consistent access to the schedule either in person or remotely.

This process takes more time at the onset, but you recoup that time by creating a realistic and streamlined understanding of dependencies and how individual team members understand their place within the whole. At the same time, you're building accountability with individual contributors. However, there is also a risk that an individual or work group may not accurately predict the length of time it takes to do their own work. Retrospectives or closeout reports from previous exhibitions might contain notes about schedule variance, which can help you either confirm or question timeline assessments.

Sometimes as you work through this planning exercise, your team will realize that you don't have enough time to complete the work within the phase dates. The collaborative schedule-making process will help to make that

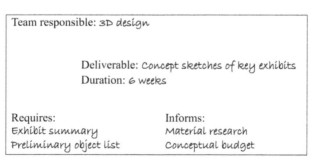

Figure 5.1 Scheduling sticky note sample

abundantly apparent because all of a sudden, a bunch of the sticky notes won't fit on the calendar. In this situation, first, ask your participants to double-check the accuracy of their durations and dependencies. If it still doesn't fit, you then have a few options:

1. Consider overlap of tasks and concurrent work
2. Shift high-impact or long-lead items to begin earlier than planned
3. Reduce the scope of the project to complete it within the allocated time
4. Phase the project deliverables
5. Extend the project timeline

The described process is just one way to engage your team in the creation of a schedule. In the end, all great schedules include major activities, durations, deadlines, and who is responsible for delivering the work. They show how work overlaps and that we all depend on each other. Whether you're using a Gantt[6] chart, a spreadsheet, or a physical calendar, we find co-creation is more useful and accurate than creating a schedule in a bubble.

WORK GROUP PLANS

While the project manager typically manages the overall project schedule by ensuring it's accurate and being updated regularly, they also might take a lead role in developing more granular work group plans. Work group plans for a design team, content team, media team, or an electrical installation team will include detailed tasks that lead to a major deliverable. Oftentimes, it takes multiple people within the same work group to complete a deliverable. A work plan, as shown in Table 5.4, can help to coordinate contributions from the person accountable for a deliverable and their collaborators.

Table 5.4 Work plan sample

Deliverable	Task	Assigned to	Date needed	Completed	Notes
Sample labels	Draft copy	Content developer	March 1	X	
	Voice and tone review	Editor	March 15	X	
	Draft approval	Director of content	April 1		
	Submit to translators	Content developer	April 7		10 days required
	Deliver final copy to graphic designer	Content developer	April 28		

Budgets and Schedules

Work plans often contain too much information for the big-picture project schedule, but it's important they are well aligned *with* the overall schedule. For that reason, project managers should be involved or at least have visibility to those detailed plans. But you'll have more success with these plans if they are created and driven by the people doing the work within them. Many software programs will allow tasks to be linked between schedules. At minimum, you'll want work group plans posted in a shared space for transparency.

WORKING SIDE BY SIDE WITH YOUR ARCHITECT
by Ed Kim

On large capital projects, you might engage an architect to support your work. Architects can help answer building code questions, design beautiful spaces, and help you get a construction permit. They should also be helping you to set realistic goals for both budget and schedule. Here are a couple key points I've learned as an architectural design project manager working on design-build teams for museums that can help your project move smoothly to fruition:

1. **Collaborate to create a holistic vision:** An integrated team structure can help align exhibit elements with the overall existing architectural space and character. Doing so can yield a more holistic visitor experience. For exhibition projects that also include remodels or entire new buildings, the museum staff, architecture firm, general contractor, and exhibit design firm should work together early on to build that holistic design and determine how choices will impact budget and schedule.
2. **Double down on transparency and communication:** Better communication between the museum team and the design-build team can reveal the complexities and potential obstacles inherent in exhibition design program goals and existing buildings, including realistic and honest schedule and budget setting. An integrated team should engage in transparent discussions regarding the complexities of exhibition design, such as the time required for research, development, fabrication, and installation.
3. **Support difficult conversations with leadership:** Supporting challenging conversations between client-side project leadership and donors can be crucial. For example, a design-build team can help effectively communicate technical project aspects to highlight the importance of a schedule or budget change to achieve the overall project vision. This way the museum staff representative is not solely responsible for communicating this information all the way up the museum hierarchy. When adjustments are needed, your architect can help by outlining

> alternate options with varying approaches to material/fabrication procurement, permitting packages, and overlapping design phasing. Prioritizing transparency and integrity in delivering outcomes, even if it means an undesired but honest outcome, is ultimately what serves the project best.

NOTES

1. A project sponsor is a designated champion *within your organization* who has a position of high influence or high enough rank to provide resources, support, critical decision-making, and advocacy on behalf of the project.
2. Chris Hendrickson, Carl Haas, and Tung Au, "Cost and Schedule Control, Monitoring and Accounting," in *Project Management for Construction (and Deconstruction)*, Pressbooks, March 1, 2024, https://ecampusontario.pressbooks.pub/projectmanagementforconstructionanddeconstruction/chapter/cost-and-schedule-control-monitoring-and-accounting/. A cost to completion is a type of construction cost control estimate that combines actual costs to date with future predicted costs.
3. Project Management Institute, *The Standard for Risk Management in Portfolios, Programs, and Projects* (Project Management Institute, Inc., 2019). Including a contingency is one aspect of risk management. More strategies can be found in Project Management Institute resources.
4. Rich Seiler, *The Pull Planning Playbook for Foreman and Superintendents: Learn the Coach's X's and O's to Pull Like Pros* (Unified Works, Inc., 2019).
5. Project Management Institute, *A Guide to the Project Management Body of Knowledge (PMBOK® Guide)*, fifth edition (Newtown Square, PA: Project Management Institute, Inc., 2013).
6. Project Management Institute, *A Guide to the Project Management Body of Knowledge*, 182–83.

6

Meeting Routines

Once you've established your project team and the essentials of budget and schedule, and held your kickoff, it's time to set up the overall project meeting structure. People want to know what's going on, participate in creative activities, and feel heard when they give feedback. That's understandable—there can be a lot of excitement and anticipation around being involved in creating something new. We often hear about meeting overload. In contrast, it's also easy to fall into the habit of canceling meetings when they are not perfectly convenient. You'll want to find the right balance and routines so that meetings amplify the energy in the room rather than drain it.

AGENDA SETTING

Crafting a clear agenda for meetings will help with efficiency, focus, and morale. Each meeting should have an articulated purpose with outcomes that are relevant to everyone in the room. Some meeting agendas should be developed in collaboration with others, and some you'll be able to craft on your own. In both cases, there should be opportunities for interaction and discussion, with time at the end for clarifying next steps and action items. Clear agendas can help a collaborative or cross-disciplinary team understand why they are present and to help the group stay focused on one topic at a time.

STATUS MEETINGS

The key to status meetings is to make them quick and consistent. To help with this, we like to use a weekly scrum routine[1] or stand-up meeting, with a routine agenda that aligns context and activities for the week. Each team member shares what they've done since the last time the group met, what they are going to do on the project between now and the next time they meet, and if they are experiencing any barriers. The idea is to update, not discuss. If discussion is warranted, it happens at the end of the meeting, or we determine that a specific meeting is needed to dig into it for resolution.

WORKING MEETINGS

In highly collaborative environments, complex deliverables will benefit from working meetings or work sessions where a few people work together to produce a single product. For instance, to create a mood board, a designer will work with a content developer and fabricator to review materials and colors and assess and test them. Working teams will need regular intervals to work on these deliverables together, and that time will need to be set aside for them within the project schedule. These meetings can easily get out of hand when too many people are invited. While we strive for an inclusive and collaborative process, we know that small, focused groups are more efficient at getting work done. In general, most project meetings and working groups should be no larger than six people for maximum efficiency.[2] You can support these work sessions by keeping the guest list to a minimum. Taking a holistic view of project priorities, you can help people understand the benefit of keeping the meeting small and focused and how the information will be shared with others as deliverables progress.

WALL-TO-WALL MEETINGS

Scheduling meetings with a large group of people can be disruptive to the workday, and it can be difficult to get everyone in the same room at the same time. One strategy that has worked for us is grouping major project meetings all together on one day. We call it Wall-to-Wall Wednesday.[3] On this day, we host major status updates, feedback sessions, charrettes, and even benchmarking research trips, leaving other days lighter on meetings and more focused on individual work time or smaller work sessions. In this model, the whole day on Wednesday is blocked off on the project team's calendar along with a consistent location. This gives everyone visibility and consistency for these meetings, access to each other and each other's work throughout the day, and unfettered time to move major collaborative efforts forward. This could be done in person, remotely, or via a hybrid format.

MEETING NOTES

Accurate and consistent meeting notes will help your team track decisions and support accountability. We find the most helpful meeting notes document decisions, actions, and next steps. Here are some strategies you can employ to make this important task a bit easier and more consistent throughout your team.

- **Start with a template.** Having a template for meeting notes is an easy way to support note-taking. A template is also a way to create consistency so people know what to expect and others can do this in the absence of a designated notetaker. Create a notes template to document decisions, actions, and next steps in a digestible format, focusing on the big takeaways that help move the work forward.
- **Encourage individual ownership and tracking of tasks.** As tasks come up during a meeting for each individual or work group, you can encourage a sense of ownership among your team members. Team members should be encouraged to document their own action items in a shared document for visibility to the whole team. This will take the burden off of one person and, instead, will distribute ownership of documenting outcomes to the project team.
- **Review action items out loud.** This is a good routine to get into, no matter the size or duration of the meeting, to develop shared understanding before the meeting breaks and everyone goes in their own direction. Leave 5 to 10 minutes at the end of your meeting and recap out loud the list of action items you recorded during the meeting. Ask if there were other action items or key points to include. These tasks can be transferred to a work plan or other task list later, as long as they have been identified and assigned. Recapping them out loud helps to summarize while it's fresh in everyone's mind.
- **Share the notes.** Sometimes even small decisions have an impact on someone's work and making notes consistently visible to others is an easy way to find this out. Sometimes that can feel unnecessary because everyone on the team was present for the meeting. But inevitably, it'll be the one meeting whose notes didn't get shared that will be the subject of questioning and misaligned memories. You can create consistency by establishing one place to share notes so that everyone knows where to look for them.
- **Designate an alternate notetaker.** While the notetaker is often the project manager, it doesn't always have to be. For some, facilitating a large meeting and note-taking at the same time can be distracting, and you might need support from a trusted colleague to take notes while you facilitate. Or, if there are meetings happening in smaller work groups without a project manager, this might lead to concern about missing information or passive decision-making. Stressing and obsessing about a meeting you're not attending is no fun. You can relieve this by designating an alternate person who *is* attending the meeting to take notes or document key decisions and takeaways in one of the formats above.

- **Establish your tech philosophy.** Decide as a team what project management software you'll use together and stick with it. Most software tools have features that can support status updates and meeting notes, often in tandem with a cloud-based file storage system. This will support on-site, remote, and hybrid team environments, ensuring transparency wherever you're at.

NOTES

1. Jeff Sutherland, *Scrum: The Art of Doing Twice the Work in Half the Time* (Crown Currency, 2014).
2. Katherine Klein, "Is Your Team Too Big? Too Small? What's the Right Number?," Knowledge at Wharton, June 14, 2006, https://knowledge.wharton.upenn.edu/podcast/knowledge-at-wharton-podcast/is-your-team-too-big-too-small-whats-the-right-number-2/.
3. University of Washington Project Delivery Group, "Meet the 2021 Design-Build Project of the Year Team," Design-Build Delivers, December 2, 2021, https://designbuilddelivers.buzzsprout.com/2084451/11706950-meet-the-2021-design-build-project-of-the-year-team.

Part 2
Creating the Vision

Creating exhibitions and generating new ideas can be fun and rewarding work. At the same time, arriving at ideas that clearly support your content goals for a specific audience, are engaging and awe-inspiring experiences, and can be built within your budget and schedule can be challenging. Creating a clear vision, in both content and design, is critical to effectively and efficiently building exhibition components, media and digital experiences, animal displays, object mounts, graphics, final copy, and all the other making and production that leads to creating excellent exhibitions.[1] You can support a clear vision through strong facilitation and by creating environments conducive to collaborative innovation *and* independent work. We'll cover strategies for both in this section.

Note

1. Beverly Serrell, *Judging Exhibitions: A Framework for Assessing Excellence* (Left Coast Press, 2006). While excellence is certainly very subjective, Beverly Serrell published a framework for judging excellence in exhibitions from a visitor-centered perspective in 2006. This publication explores and explains the framework, along with the story of how this framework came to be.

7
Facilitation

Facilitating creative work to come up with impactful, relevant, beautiful, and feasible exhibits is one of the great joys of working on collaborative teams. This work is fun. And it needs to be carefully thought out to help your team build positive relationships, focus, and keep your project moving forward. Creative work and facilitating creative work also require some level of vulnerability.[1] Participants must be willing to share ideas, hear feedback, change their mind, and change their work as a result.[2] Not everyone has practice in this so it's important to set up structures that support openness and trust among team members.

FACILITATING CREATIVITY

Facilitation is the practice of supporting groups working together in a positive, generative, and efficient way. Facilitators are advocates of structures and routines that serve the group and encourage discussion and collaboration between each person.[3] While a project manager can act as the facilitator for creative work, sometimes a content developer or designer will facilitate idea generation and refinement. In other structures, someone outside the project, like a consultant, will act as the facilitator. In any case, there are several key points that facilitators should keep top of mind:

- **Great ideas can come from a variety of sources.** Everyone comes to this work from different avenues, and a good facilitator values and celebrates those differences and invites them into a shared space.
- **Co-creation means designing and developing *with* your collaborators.**[4] Co-creation should start at the earliest phases of your exhibit project.

As you consider which meetings, processes, and tools to use for creative development, you can (and should) be an advocate for ensuring users, community members, operational team members, maintenance staff, and other diverse voices have an opportunity to contribute to the exhibition-making process.

- **People need quiet, independent thinking time *and* collaborative work time.** When developing activities and agendas for idea generation, it's important to include time for both independent and collaborative work. We recommend taking multiple consecutive days for creative activities. Having several days to focus on a topic and nights to sleep on ideas and process major decisions may help people who appreciate more time to think things through.
- **The setting, agenda, and tools need to support productive work.** Take note of what works well for your team to do their best work. We find that rooms with natural light, a variety of food, and easy access to hydration and coffee support the sustained energy needed for longer meetings. Asking your team what they need can help you iterate on how you set them up for success.
- **A truly neutral facilitator is rare.** If you're the project manager on the team and are also facilitating creative development workshops, you probably aren't neutral. You've likely spent time understanding the content, have a strong familiarity with the exhibition space, and know what works for your organization's audiences. You may also have a background as a designer, developer, educator, or fabricator. While it might make sense for you to abstain from offering strong opinions or ideas in some situations, make sure you participate fully in others. It helps to be clear when you're taking off your "facilitator hat" and contributing based on expertise.

CREATIVE OPENERS

The purpose of creative openers is to practice developing and sharing in preparation for idea generation. These openers are often a bit silly to loosen people up and allow for connection ahead of longer creative design sessions. They should be short and sweet, hopefully with some laughter sprinkled in. Depending on your work culture, activities like this can sometimes be dismissed as a waste of time, especially if they're not used intentionally. But it's important to take time to plan and facilitate openers aligned to the goals for the day to set the tone for successful creative work. Low-stakes activities like this are also key to building relationships and trust, which are the foundation of collaborative work. Here are some of our go-to creative openers:

1. **30 Circles:** Provide each participant with a sheet of paper that has 30 small circles on it.[5] Give them three minutes to draw something different in each circle, asking people to turn each circle into a recognizable thing. For exhibition making, we like to use prompts that relate to a specific topic. For example, draw something ocean related, draw something con-  nected to nature, or draw something related to your typical daily routines in each circle. At some point, most people will get stumped and think they're out of ideas. Given some encouragement from a facilitator, they'll be able to come up with a few more ideas, inspiring confidence before they begin brainstorming exhibit ideas.

2. **Tape It Up:** Each participant writes the name of an animal or object on a small piece of paper. They put the papers into a bowl, and each person selects one at random without show- ing others. Then, everyone gets three minutes to create whatever was put on their piece of paper using only masking tape.[6] After three minutes, each person shares their creation, and the group tries to guess what it 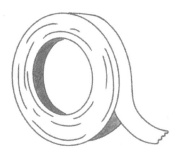 is. If people guess correctly, it will build confidence in the maker's abilities; if they don't guess correctly, it becomes a funny way to embrace a bit of low-stakes failure.

3. **Squiggle Bird:** Give each participant a piece of paper and three seconds to make four small scribbles on it. Each person then exchanges their paper with someone else and, with a differ- ent colored pen or pencil, they turn those scribbles into birds.[7] There are easy metaphors here about making something out of nothing and finding patterns in the chaos.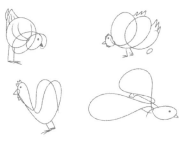

4. **Draw Your Neighbor:** Ask everyone to turn to a partner and draw their face in two minutes without looking at their paper or lifting their pencil.[8] This results in abstract drawings of each person and loosens the expectation for refined drawings during  idea generation. This is also an opportunity to reflect on the power of observation. We sometimes do these drawings on sticky notes and then make a "class photo," posting them on the board for the duration of the workshop.
5. **Word Association:** This activity doesn't require any materials, but it does require everyone to talk out loud in the group. Everyone stands in a circle, and someone starts by saying a word. The next person says the first word that popped into their head when they heard the previous word. This continues around the circle. When it gets back to the person who started, they have to share how the last word is connected to the first word. Finding a connection between two seemingly random words can inspire confidence in building on each other's ideas.
6. **Paper Clips:** The group stands in a circle, and the first person holds a paper clip or other common object. They describe a use for that object; then they pass it to the next person, who shares a different use for that object. If you use a paper clip or something similarly pliable, participants can change the shape as it goes around the circle. The key is to not repeat  a use someone has already said. Continue at least once fully around the circle or up to three times around. This activity encourages people to look beyond their first round of ideas.

READING THE ROOM

In addition to creative development activities, the facilitator's most important role is knowing how to pivot when the group needs something different. To do this, you'll need to be both self-aware and attuned to the needs, attitudes, and opinions of other people. You'll probably see moments of your team humming along during creative facilitation, and you'll also see them getting stuck. Keep in mind that not all struggles are negative.[9] A team will need to work through ideas and conflicts during creative development to arrive at meaningful outcomes. It's your role as a facilitator to see all of this and to know when to support, when to shift, and when to encourage the team to keep going. As you observe and reflect, here are common questions you might have, along with possible ways to address them as a facilitator:

- **Is the room too quiet?** They might need a break, or they might need food.
- **Is the same person dominating a conversation, or is the loudest voice in the room persuading others to follow their direction?** Switch up a whole-group conversation into smaller groups or pairs.
- **Are some people resistant to sharing ideas or feedback out loud?** Consider shifting to sticky notes and asking the group to write out their ideas.
- **Are participants not even close to completing the activity in the time you allotted?** Think about what can be cut to allow time to meet the true goal of the meeting rather than rushing through a meaningful activity.
- **Did you ask the group a question only to be met with silence?** Take a long sip of water to make room for others to process and contribute.
- **Are you talking too much?** Self-awareness is key for this one! Try moving to the back of the room to help signal that others should take the lead in the conversation.

Strategies for facilitation aren't unique to the museum or exhibition field, so if this is a newer role for you, find a partner and practice. We've found that some of our most attuned facilitators have backgrounds in teaching or presenting. Collaborative exhibition making is a great opportunity for those who want to learn this work and might have a skill set or natural talent to do so. The more competent facilitators you have on your team, the more you'll be able to take turns between facilitating and participating. Learning to read the room takes time, and large groups of people have complex needs. So be ready to iterate on your facilitation style. Ask your participants for honest feedback so you know what to try out next time.

NOTES

1. Ashish Goel and Stanford d.school, *Drawing on Courage: Risks Worth Taking and Stands Worth Making* (Berkeley, CA: Ten Speed Press, 2022). Most people will likely feel vulnerable or will need to try or learn something new at some point during creative work and facilitation. For additional practices on building courage using design principles, we recommend this delightful read.
2. Scott Doorley, Carissa Carter, and Stanford d.school, *Assembling Tomorrow: A Guide to Designing a Thriving Future* (Berkeley, CA: Ten Speed Press, 2024), 157-90. "Design is a process of discovery. Ideas begin, remedies come out of hiding, and opportunities step into the light only when you take the time to sit with and question things. Uncovering gaps like this takes discipline—it asks you to look at trouble to reveal possibility. To even begin to discover what's been overlooked, you have to examine everything, even the parts you didn't think were part of it. The work can be boring and tedious or unsettling and

awkward. You have to push against your instincts to ignore the familiar, your impatience to move on, and your uncertainty about what may or may not be useful" (188).
3. Robert J. Garmston and Bruce M. Wellman, *The Adaptive School: A Sourcebook for Developing Collaborative Groups* (Lanham, MD: Rowman & Littlefield, 2016), 95–111. For additional resources on facilitating collaborative groups, we recommend reading Chapter 7, "The Confident and Skilled Facilitator."
4. When Dr. Elin Kelsey was working with us on designing a program, she described co-creation as *"when the product is different because you were there. Which means the product is different because each individual person was there. And without any one of them, the product would be, again, different."*
5. Thomas Kelley and David Kelley, *Creative Confidence: Unleashing the Creative Potential within Us All* (New York: Crown Publishing Group, 2013), 219–21.
6. Tape It Up was inspired from seeing the work of artist Danny Scheible, creator of Tapigami, at Maker Faire, who creates large-scale collaborative sculptures using masking tape.
7. Dave Gray, "Squiggle Birds," Gamestorming, February 27, 2015, https://gamestorming.com/squiggle-birds/.
8. Kimon Nicolaïdes, *The Natural Way to Draw: A Working Plan for Art Study* (Houghton Mifflin, 1941); Sarah Stein Greenberg and Stanford d.school, *Creative Acts for Curious People: How to Think, Create, and Lead in Unconventional Ways* (Berkeley, CA: Ten Speed Press, 2021), 30–31. Drawing a subject without looking at your paper is a classic artists' practice called a blind contour. Greenberg describes using the practice as an activity to *"shortcut the distance between the eye and the hand."*
9. Greenberg and Stanford d.school, *Creative Acts for Curious People*, 206–11. Greenberg describes productive struggle as the *"experience in between the bright possibility of a breakthrough and being off-balance while struggling to get there."*

8

Creative Development

We think of creative development as the process of imagining, generating, refining, and communicating ideas. Since exhibitions are visitor centered and require the work of many different disciplines to make, creative development should be done both collaboratively and independently.[1] We often find that creative development is focused on idea generation, but generating new ideas over and over will keep your team stuck in the concept phase. Idea generation can't move a project forward unless it's refined and documented and can be shared with others for feedback and input. So, in addition to idea generation, we've included strategies for creating a basis of design, refining ideas, summarizing exhibit ideas, understanding and supporting visual communication, and phasing design documentation. The strategies in this chapter can be used for all types of ideas. We use the general term "exhibit idea" for consistency here, but you could use the same strategies to create the big idea, refine content messaging, design interactive or media elements, or even brainstorm and decide on the title of your exhibition.

BASIS OF DESIGN

You'll need to define the creative intent and creative guardrails for your team. Sometimes this is also called a creative brief, design brief, or design intent. In architectural terms, this is often called a *basis of design*, which is a technical report that includes standards and criteria for different building systems. A basis of design for an exhibition project can serve as the underlying guidance for creative direction, decisions, coordination, and alignment. For exhibitions, we like to include creative standards and strategies depending on how firmly they are held by your team and organization. The process for developing a basis of design is similar to the project brief: gather information by asking questions and performing research, sort the information, and share and review.

Defining your basis of design early, in either the planning or concept phases, will help to guide and align creative direction and idea generation. This can apply to content development as well as exhibit and experience design and will extend all the way through engaging contractors, fabrication, and construction. A basis of design will represent standards and values held by your organization, such as how you prioritize sustainability. Other strategies will be more specifically related to a certain project, such as the intended audience. As you articulate a basis of design for an exhibition project, you should also be asking:

- How does this project fit within your existing vision, audience, branding, interpretive approach, and look and feel as an organization?
- Where can this project diverge or not diverge from existing standards?

The more clarity you can provide in your standards and strategies within a basis of design, the better you'll be able to use it for guidance, decision-making, and alignment along the way.

Below are categories included in a basis of design with excerpts of sample language.[2] When creating your own, you should add and remove categories based on your own needs. You should include standards or strategies that you can stand behind, which in some cases may be quite minimal and direct, so that when it comes to creative development, you're moving forward rather than backward.

- **Vision**

    A cohesive description of what you envision as the north star for the creative team, such as *We will create a welcoming space for particular needs of our younger audiences (ages two to eight) and their adult caregivers. We strive for elegance and simplicity, embracing negative space. Exhibit components should be inviting and intuitive to use, requiring minimal or no instructions.*

- **Interpretive Approach**

    The approach and tone you'll use for interpretation and content development, such as *Our exhibition will welcome children and their caregivers with a playful, friendly voice and a conversational tone. Interpretive elements will use informal, child-friendly language for adults to easily read aloud to their little ones and will be fully bilingual in English and Spanish.*

- **Look and Feel**

    While you may not know all the details of look and feel yet, this is a place to set the foundation of this exploration, such as *We are drawn to the warmth of natural materials and a color palette inspired by nature.*

- **Accessibility**

    Articulate your organization's overall philosophy on accessibility[3] and how accessibility priorities are incorporated into your project, for example, *We seek to weave accessibility for all visitors into the fabric of experience design. All designed components should meet the highest accessibility standards. Graphics should employ a readable typeface and colors that offer high contrast. Any interactive elements should be operable with a closed fist.* Include specific accessibility strategies[4] with respect to audiences, such as including braille or other strategies for blind or low-sighted visitors, wheelchair accessibility, and other apparent or unapparent disabilities.[5]

- **Seating**

    Seating and rest are critical aspects of any visitor experience,[6] so we like to include thoughts about seating and how to prioritize basic visitor needs right up front in planning stages. Here's an example: *Abundant, comfortable seating should be available throughout the gallery. Caregivers should feel welcome to rest, to nurse, to hold a small child while an older child plays. Seating should offer multiple views so a caregiver can keep an eye on children in more than one area at a time. Some seating should provide adjacency to wheelchairs and armrests.*

- **Materials and Maintenance**

    Include specific goals related to maintainability, longevity, sustainability,[7] and any technical specifications or standards that must be followed, for example, on sustainability, *In choosing materials, we prefer timeless over trendy and celebrate inherent qualities—wood handrails, etched glass, the natural patina of brass and bronze. We choose materials with sustainability in mind, and we consider the full life cycle of the materials we use. We also recognize that sustainability can mean choosing highly durable materials that require less frequent replacement because they withstand the impacts of visitors and the rigor of cleaning and sanitizing over time.*

IDEA GENERATION

Idea generation for exhibitions is generally referred to as blue-sky brainstorming[8] and is typical in the early concept phase of your project. You may already have some parameters such as a big idea, main messages, and exhibition or space constraints to consider, but, generally, out-of-the-box thinking is highly encouraged. Sometimes ideas from these sessions aren't always feasible, and that's fine. Often, they spark new ideas that you can build on later. The participant list for blue-sky brainstorming should be expansive. Unique ideas often come from groups with the broadest possible lived experiences and expertise. We recommend blue-sky brainstorming and idea generation through facilitated charrettes.

Charrettes bring together a large group of people to generate ideas in a finite period of time.[9] They are typically full-day or multiple-day endeavors that include interdisciplinary staff, users, and consultants. You'll want a variety of perspectives and experiences in the room.[10] While idea generation is the main goal, team building can be a secondary goal of these sessions. With this in mind, we typically begin planning a charrette by asking ourselves a series of questions:

- What do we need out of this charrette to move our work forward?
- Who should be in the room? Are users included?
- How will you ensure all participants feel welcome to share their ideas?
- What information (research, content, constraints) does the group need to participate in a meaningful way?
- How will we meet the basic needs of the participants throughout each day? This includes thinking about room size, accessibility, food, breaks, restrooms, natural light, coffee, water, seating, transportation, compensation, and opportunities to reflect and provide feedback at the end of a charrette.

Here is one way to sequence large team brainstorming activities for a charrette:

1. **Set the stage.** Share guidelines for brainstorming.[11]
   a. Defer judgment
   b. Build on the ideas of others
   c. Stay focused on the topic
   d. Be visual
   e. Go for quantity
   f. Everyone has a voice
2. **Spark creativity.** Select a creative opener activity from Chapter 7 to help your participants get in the right mindset.
3. **Clarify the goal.** Provide background for the project, the big idea, any relevant main messages, and the specific charrette goal.
4. **Wild Fours.** Provide each participant with an 11- by 17-inch paper. Fold it in half twice (into quarters) and open it back up, leaving you with four rectangles on the paper.[12] As facilitator, give the group one minute per rectangle to come up with and sketch a different idea related to the topic you set forth. An example is shown in figure 8.1. You can do this multiple times with variations or additional constraints as needed. Your participants may have arrived preloaded with their ideas, and this activity helps them stretch thinking toward new ideas.

5. **Pair-Share.** Pair up participants. Ask them to share their four ideas with each other and discuss themes or ideas that really sparked their interest and connection to the charrette goal. Match two pairs together (now in a group of four) and have them share a summary of their conversation with each other. Then have the groups of four again identify any commonalities or ideas they're really excited about exploring more of.
6. **Create!** Task the teams of four with co-creation. Have them draw one idea together on a large piece of paper. This can be one of the individual ideas from Wild Fours, a combination of ideas, or an entirely new idea. It can be difficult for teams to focus on one idea, but that's their charge. If they have extra time, they can draw a second one. Provide a certain amount of time to do this (usually 20 to 30 minutes is sufficient for each idea).
7. **Share and collect feedback.** A representative from each group shares their idea with the larger audience. As they present, the other participants write their feedback on sticky notes. They then post the feedback onto the idea for the project team to take into consideration if this idea moves into refinement.
8. **Appreciation and reflection.** Finish the day asking folks to give appreciation to their group members and to provide you with feedback on the charrette workshop itself. Label one large piece of paper "Gots" and another "Needs" and ask participants to use sticky notes to add to each. This allows participants to share what they *got* out of the workshop and what they might *need* if they were to come to another one, which will help you iterate and plan future charrettes.

Figure 8.1 Wild Fours example

Creative Development

Your project team will need to assess all the ideas and do creative editing to decide which ideas move forward. You may find some ideas are inspiration for new ideas or that a combination of two ideas together begins to make sense. Selecting ideas will be based on how well connected they are to your big idea, messaging, intended audience, and other project-specific requirements in your project brief and basis of design.

You may generate some big-picture, highly innovative ideas through charrettes. This is fantastic! For these types of ideas to be successful, their clarity of vision and design documentation must be prioritized, defined, and front-loaded in the project. If big, innovative, ideas remain unclear (and unbudgeted) through subsequent phases, you're unlikely to achieve them.

REFINING IDEAS

Idea refinement happens in concept, schematic, final design, *and* fabrication. While you don't want to stay in blue-sky thinking throughout a project, refinement still requires new ideas, novel solutions, and generative thinking. And the refinement gets finer and more precise at each phase. How much or how little your team works collaboratively or independently during idea refinement will entirely depend on your team and the project phase. We typically include a variety of voices in early phases and a smaller group of people with more specific expertise as you get closer and closer to fabrication and construction.

Idea refinement generally requires four things to be successful:

1. **Designate a working team.** Refinement is typically done in smaller groups than idea generation. This is because you'll need specific expertise to make refinements that lead toward fabrication and making. The in-depth, often technical, conversations required to make clear decisions about refinement are more effective with fewer people in the room.
2. **Clear the calendar.** Remove meeting obligations for a specific period of time to allow a small creative team to focus their work at critical moments. If you really need to move an idea forward, build a mock-up or prototype, or test with an audience, a clear calendar will support team members' diving deep into creating solutions. For this to be successful, you'll need to establish a specific start and stop so they know when to come back up for air.
3. **Create a goal.** Create one clear goal for a small team to refine or develop an idea. This goal may take one day, a few days, or several weeks. The important thing is to address one goal at a time and use that goal to refine and make clear decisions, for example, *Generate three design sketches for the exhibition title wall, one of which should include a digital component. Recommend which of these ideas should move forward, identifying how it supports our basis of design and the big idea for the exhibition.*

4. **Share progress, results, and recommendations.** Designate up front how a smaller team working on idea refinement will share their work for feedback, input, decision-making, and visibility to the rest of the team. Establish a timeline for sharing results or recommendations. If work that a smaller team committed to for idea refinement is not complete within the designated timeline, stick to the timeline established for sharing with the rest of the project team. Review the progress that was made and assess if more time is needed *or* if it's decision-making that's needed.

Below are strategies for exhibition idea refinement:

- **Design sprint:** A design sprint is a structured and focused weeklong session to rapidly transition from idea to solution or to refine an existing idea. We've utilized the sprint structure to support teams' refining or problem-solving a particular exhibit component. In a design sprint, a team of no more than six participants will work together over five days to consult experts in the topic at hand, sketch ideas, decide which ideas move forward, prototype them, test them, and share results and recommendations with the larger team at the end. This rapid cycle can be used to quickly narrow the field of exploration on some of the more complicated design aspects of a project.[13]
- **Feasible Fours:** Use the same format as the Wild Fours activity in idea generation but make the ideas entirely feasible. We like to include fabricators and makers in this refinement activity because they'll be able to take a wild idea and refine it to something they know they can make using their own expertise. Share these ideas with the team using the Excite, Build, Consider (EBC) feedback strategy in Chapter 10, and you'll likely end up somewhere in between a wild and a feasible idea.
- **Tricycle refinement:** Designate a group of three team members, typically a content developer, designer, and maker (fabricator, media specialist, or model maker), to take one idea and create a drawing and written summary of the experience together. One of them should lead the process (the front wheel of the tricycle), and the other two should support and collaborate (the two back wheels), all moving together in the same direction and sharing their result with the project team.
- **Prototype and test:** A small group or even just a pairing of project team members prototype an idea, try it out, tinker with it, test with intended audiences, and share results and recommendations. Prototyping and testing are some of the most useful ways to understand if an idea is working as intended. See Chapter 9 for more strategies on prototyping and testing.
- **Independent work:** Ensure that content developers, designers, prototypers, producers, makers, and contractors all have ample time for independent work. Not all creative development, idea generation, or refinement will happen in groups. This doesn't mean it's not part of a collaborative

process. You can ensure independent work on idea refinement is aligned with the overall project by asking team members to articulate their goals and designate dates for sharing, review, and feedback.
- **Workgroup intensive:** Allocate and preserve uninterrupted time for a small discipline-focused group to work together to refine, solve, or try something that will move an exhibit idea forward. For example, allocate four weeks for a group of exhibit designers to describe and define an exhibit element through visual communication, then share with the project team for feedback. Or focus a team of exhibit fabricators on building functional prototypes and testing them together over several months, sharing progress, results, and recommendations with the larger project team along the way.

EXHIBIT SUMMARIES

As you refine and filter ideas, you'll want to begin clear documentation of what's moving forward in a simple and understandable format. We do this in the form of exhibit summaries often written by content developers, or product leads, in collaboration with educators, curators, designers, project managers, or other specialists on the team. The core of an exhibit summary is a narrative of your idea that describes how it is connected to the big idea and main messages of the overall exhibition. At each phase of creative development, you can use an exhibit summary to ground and assess ideas based on the content, interpretive, educational, and experience goals.

An exhibit summary is a living document and is quite iterative. As design and prototyping progress, the exhibit summary gets updated. As decisions are made and things change, the exhibit summary gets clarified. At the end of each phase, an exhibit summary and its corresponding design documentation should match. We find an exhibit summary to be a critical document for everything that comes next and ultimately creating an exhibition. We've included a sample exhibit summary in Table 8.1.[14]

VISUAL COMMUNICATION

The value of clear visual communication and design documentation for an exhibition project cannot be overstated. A designer or a design team will be able to visually communicate ideas and document exhibition design for the team. This can be done through precedent images, hand sketches, scale models, and storyboards,[15] all the way to three-dimensional digital models and highly detailed drawings for construction. Visual communication can be used to edit and focus exhibit ideas; synthesize many ideas into one solution; progress ideas from one phase to another; and document decisions and details for approval, estimating, and fabrication. Many team members on an exhibition team will need visual communication to understand ideas, provide feedback, and do their own work in relation to the idea.

Table 8.1 Exhibit summary sample

Project	Ocean Habitats Gallery
Date	[date]
Created by	Lead content developer
Exhibition big idea	Animals in the bay live in a variety of habitats that are worth protecting.
Exhibition area	Shale reef
Featured animal	Skeleton shrimp (*Caprella* spp.)
Primary messages	• For camouflage, skeleton shrimp are adapted to look like algae. • Skeleton shrimp feed by grabbing passing food with their "claws."
Summary description	A circular window offers a view onto a colorful jumble of swaying anemones and rocks covered in pink and orange algae. A magnifying lens in front of the window cues you that there is something to see if you look more closely. Text on an adjacent panel tells you that what you'll see is a tiny shrimp, called a skeleton shrimp, that is well camouflaged because it's the same color as the algae in its environment. A photo of the shrimp on the graphic panel helps you understand what to look for, and as you move the magnifier in front of the window, you spot the shrimp sitting on a rock. The label also tells you how the shrimp feeds by snagging passing food with its "claws." The shrimp you've discovered isn't feeding right now, but next to the exhibit, a video shows you this behavior so you can see it for yourself.
Exhibit elements	• Live-animal exhibit featuring skeleton shrimp in a realistic rockwork habitat accompanied by algae and anemones • Animal ID label • Close-up photo of skeleton shrimp • Magnifier lens in front of animal exhibit that visitors can manipulate • Video monitor with video showing skeleton shrimp feeding
Visitor experience goals this supports	• Seeing animals in realistic natural environments • Looking closely and making rewarding discoveries
Need to clarify	• Does the visitor start the video, or does it run in a loop? • Magnifiers can be frustrating if it's too hard to find the thing you're looking for—definitely prototype this.

Creative Development

There are a few things you can do to support designers' producing this work *within* the overall expectations of your project. If you're contracting design work, this is information you'll provide to them. If you have an in-house design team, this would be information you clarify and align together.

- Identify a clear scope of work to be accomplished.
- Provide the most current exhibit descriptions and goals through exhibit summaries and basis of design.
- Identify, share, and ensure access to design-specific goals from the project brief or existing documentation (accessibility, sustainability, capacity for visitors, coordination with existing conditions, considerations to be resolved, and constraints).
- Identify a clear schedule for completion of major deliverables with enough time to evaluate feasibility, budget, and schedule prior to the end of a phase.
- Clarify who will be providing feedback on design and when and how that will happen as well as who will make final design decisions.
- Set up clear processes and points of contact so all team members can be responsive to questions, inquiries, and clarifications.
- Support your team in being willing to change their minds based on input and expertise from your designer.

As one designer recently put it, "each day, your idea has to be better than it was the day before"[16] for design to progress. That's a lot of pressure. Be aware of this and set expectations for yourself and the rest of your team. Anticipate time in your schedule for some flexibility in design so they can move through moments of rethinking. At the same time, notice when a designer is being asked to iterate something over and over without resolution. This could mean your goals are not clear to begin with or expectations are unrealistic. Working with and supporting designers is a large part of the development and refinement process. Creating appropriate expectations and processes around this work will help you entrust designers to lead independent design and idea generation more successfully and in service to the whole project.

DESIGN DOCUMENTATION

Design documentation at each phase should build on the prior documentation with subsequently more detail and specifications, ultimately leading to physical or digital[17] fabrication and installation that meets your criteria and intent. At earlier phases, this will be used for feedback and approval and, at later phases, for fabrication, permitting, construction, and keeping track of real conditions and changes. Table 8.2 includes general guidance on the type of

Table 8.2 Design documentation by phase

Project phase	Design deliverables	What the deliverable documents
Planning	• As-built drawings, floor plans, and elevations of existing exhibition space	• Existing conditions and constraints
Concept	• Bubble diagrams • Preliminary floor plans • Sketches • Renderings • Precedent images • Mood board • Sample graphic designs	• Content relationships • Massing and circulation • Potential exhibit elements • Look and feel • Design intent • Material exploration • Graphic strategy
Schematic	• Floor plans • Renderings, perspective drawings, digital or physical model • Material sample boards • Elevations • Storyboards	• Spatial organization • Elements and locations • Material intent • Graphic and object sizes and locations • Media experiences
Final design	• Detailed drawings and renderings • Graphic design files • Final floor plans; wall elevations; reflected ceiling plans; electrical, lighting, and data plans	• Dimensions, media, and fabrication methods for each element • Signs and labels • Architectural integration
Fabrication and construction	• Construction drawings and shop drawings • Control documentation • Graphic production files	• Dimensions, materials, finishes, hardware, software • Specifications and standards • Final graphics for print
Installation and completion	• As-built drawings or redlines • Operations and maintenance manuals • Photo documentation of completed exhibition	• Errors, changes, and revisions • Training, maintenance procedures, and warranties • Confirmation of completion

design deliverables at each phase of exhibition making and what the deliverables document for the project.[18] This will vary with the scope and complexity of your project.

We've included a sampling of design snippets in Figures 8.2 through 8.7 so you can see the progression and refinement of design documentation and visual communication through exhibition-making phases.[19]

Figure 8.2 Concept Sketch example

Figure 8.3 Concept rendering example

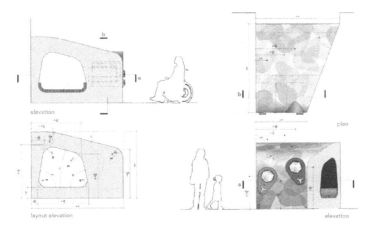

Figure 8.4 Schematic with dimensions example

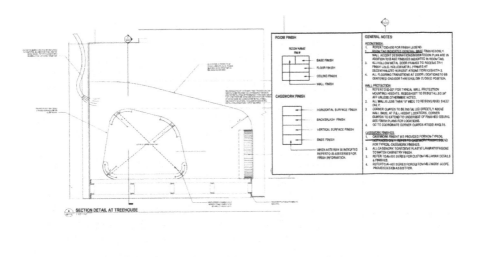

Figure 8.5 Final design drawing example

Creative Development

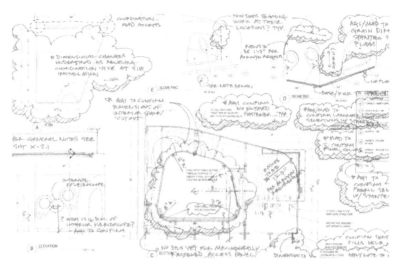

Figure 8.6 Shop drawings with notations

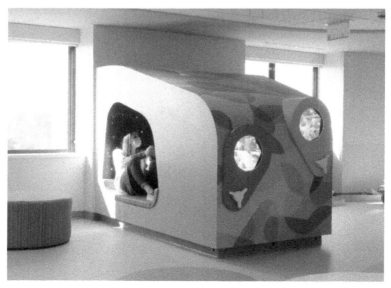

Figure 8.7 Photo of final fabrication

NOTES

1. Naomi Crellin and Lauren Telchin Katz, "Design-Thinking Approaches to Exhibition Development: Investigating New Ways of Working," *Exhibition: A Journal of Exhibition Theory & Practice for Museum Professionals* 38, no. 1 (Spring 2019), https://www.aam-us.org/wp-content/uploads/2024/04/14_Exhibition_DesignThinkingApproachesToExhibitionDevelopment.pdf. Crellin and Katz describe a case study of adapting design-thinking strategies (sprint and agile structures) for managing and designing collaborative exhibitions and creative development processes for the Smithsonian Institution's National Museum of American History (NMAH): *In Sickness and In Health* Exhibition.
2. Sample excerpts for the basis of design are edited from a design strategies document created by a collaborative project team at the Monterey Bay Aquarium in 2024.
3. Maria Chiara Ciaccheri, *Museum Accessibility by Design: A Systemic Approach to Organizational Change* (Lanham, MD: Rowman & Littlefield, 2022). Recommended further reading on accessibility within museums, including some of the barriers and practical guidance to developing organizational solutions.
4. "The Americans with Disabilities Act," ADA.gov, May 22, 2024, https://www.ada.gov/. *"The Americans with Disabilities Act (ADA) protects people with disabilities from discrimination."* "About Universal Design," Centre for Excellence in Universal Design, accessed October 17, 2024, https://universaldesign.ie/about-universal-design. *"Universal design (UD) is the design and composition of an environment so that it can be accessed, understood, and used to the greatest extent possible by all people regardless of their age, size, ability, or disability."* Your organization and project team should be specific about how you are meeting and exceeding accessibility for visitor-centered design of exhibitions.
5. Beth Redmond-Jones, *Welcoming Museum Visitors with Unapparent Disabilities* (Lanham, MD: Rowman & Littlefield, 2024). Recommended further reading on unapparent disabilities.
6. Elissa Frankle Olinsky, "Maslow in Museums," frankleolinsky.com, accessed October 17, 2024, https://www.frankleolinsky.com/maslow-in-museums.
7. "Sustainable Exhibition Design & Construction Toolkit," American Alliance of Museums, accessed June 20, 2023, https://www.aam-us.org/2023/06/20/sustainable-exhibition-design-construction-toolkit/?gad_source=1&gclid=CjwKCAjwqMO0BhA8EiwAFTLgID8Fn2kQ3ouRFMsmLJNmPiaRQzRdgulaTQQaVa-c04ljxbXkUmdGrRoCRI8QAvD_BwE. MuseumNext and the American Alliance of Museums provide resources and information on sustainability in museums, and sustainable exhibition design and construction. We recommend using these resources as a starting point for understanding sustainability within your own organization and to create your own statements regarding organizational commitment and vision toward sustainability that you will use for guidance and decision-making during design and construction.
8. Tim Brown and Barry Martin Katz, *Change by Design: How Design Thinking Transforms Organizations and Inspires Innovation* (New York: HarperCollins, 2019), 69–92. Recommended further reading on the process and value of brainstorming to create

ideas from a whole organizational perspective as well as using sticky notes to make choices on ideas.
9. Polly McKenna-Cress and Janet A. Kamien, *Creating Exhibitions: Collaboration in the Planning, Development, and Design of Innovative Experiences* (Hoboken, NJ: John Wiley & Sons, Inc., 2013), 54.
10. Tania Anaissie et al., "Liberatory Design," Liberatory Design, accessed July 12, 2024, https://www.liberatorydesign.com/.
11. "What is Brainstorming?," IDEO U, accessed October 17, 2024, https://www.ideou.com/pages/brainstorming.
12. Jake Knapp, John Zeratsky, and Braden Kowitz, *Sprint: How to Solve Big Problems and Test New Ideas in Just Five Days* (New York: Simon & Schuster, 2016), 111-13. Wild Fours, based on the activity Crazy Eights in the book *Sprint*, was adapted and renamed in 2017 by a collaborative team in the Education Division at the Monterey Bay Aquarium.
13. Knapp et al., *Sprint*.
14. The exhibit summary format was created by Erica Kelly. The sample provided is based on an existing exhibition at the Monterey Bay Aquarium.
15. Ellen Lupton, *Design Is Storytelling* (Washington, DC: Cooper Hewitt, 2017), 34-39. Storyboards tell stories through a sequence of images that might represent a film, a multimedia interactive, or another type of experience. *"The purpose of a storyboard is to explain action with a concise series of pictures."*
16. Jason Manning, in conversation with the authors, June 5, 2024.
17. Barry Joseph, *Making Dinosaurs Dance: A Toolkit for Digital Design in Museums* (Lanham, MD: Rowman & Littlefield, 2023). Digital fabrication can include original film and video, on-screen or projected media, programming, and interactive exhibits and components.
18. Polly McKenna-Cress and Janet A. Kamien, *Creating Exhibitions: Collaboration in the Planning, Development, and Design of Innovative Experiences* (Hoboken, NJ: John Wiley & Sons, Inc., 2013), 270-85; Barry Lord, Gail Dexter Lord, and Lindsay Martin, *Manual of Museum Planning: Sustainable Space, Facilities, and Operations*, third edition (Lanham, MD: AltaMira Press, 2012), 95-96; Kathleen McLean, *Planning for People in Museum Exhibitions* (Washington, DC: Association of Science and Technology Centers, 1993), 60-65. Design documentation by phase is a combination of exhibit-making processes as we've experienced them, as well as a combination of several foundational exhibition planning, development, and design texts.
19. Design documentation examples in Figures 8.2-8.7 were provided courtesy of Jason Manning and Metcalfe Architecture & Design.

9
Prototyping

Prototyping brings ideas off the page, out of a digital model, and into the real world. Often, when we reference prototyping in exhibition work,[1] we are talking about a physical or interactive element being tested with visitors. There are many ways to think about prototyping throughout an exhibition project. A prototype is a "tool that gives you a chance to investigate your ideas and explore what could, should, or would come next."[2] And it should be "both iterative and reductive, getting better and simpler along the way."[3] Unfortunately, it's often squeezed out of project budgets and timelines.[4] We've found that establishing some structure to prototyping is helpful to determine when and what to prototype so that your team can use this time wisely.

PRIORITIZE PROTOTYPING

Once your team experiences the positive impact of exhibit prototyping, they'll want to prototype *everything*. That could lead to building almost the entire exhibit two times over, and you likely won't have time for that. You'll need to prioritize. Begin by creating a prototyping list so that you can see the full suite of exhibit ideas or elements that would benefit from prototyping.[5] Think about the entire project as you create this list. If you don't, you might end up prototyping whatever comes up first, and you'll run out of time or resources to prototype other major elements down the road. Ideas and elements that rise to the top will typically be high-risk components or novel ideas with usability concerns.

Using this list, ask yourselves this question about each exhibit idea or item on the list: *What is the one thing that, if missing, would make the exhibit idea fail?* This will lead you to identify the most critical piece of information that needs to be prototyped first and resolved before the idea can move forward.

It helps to have staff dedicated to prototyping so that you can prototype whenever you need. What a dream! But we also know that's rare. Fortunately, prototyping can be built into all our job descriptions in different capacities. It's informed *and* performed by content developers, designers, fabricators, project managers, media developers, and on and on at all phases of exhibition making. The more people who are involved in tinkering and testing ideas, the more ownership and investment you'll have in the result.

As you create a prototyping plan, designate who is making the prototype, who they are testing with, and how they will share results with the team (Table 9.1). A prototyping plan is rarely going to be one and done, as you will gain information from each prototype to inform new variations. A prototyping plan should be a living document. Use it to record results, share photos and video, and document decisions and outcomes. This information will inform new decisions and next steps.

Creating and using shared terminology for prototyping will also help you prioritize and more clearly identify what you're aiming to achieve with each effort. If you're trying to validate how something works, for example, you might need a full mechanical prototype at an early stage. However, if you're trying to decide how something looks, you might need swatches and samples to test with existing lighting conditions. Creating shared terminology around the motivation and utility of prototyping will help you create structure and purpose to what you do and how you use your time and resources doing it. Table 9.2 shows an example of shared terminology for prototyping.[6]

WHEN AND WHAT TO PROTOTYPE

Prototyping can be a simple paper mock-up to place objects in a diorama, words on paper to represent a digital interactive, tape and cardboard to block out spatial relationships, or sample graphics, *all the way to* complex digital and physical pilot products to test for accessibility, usability, safety, and maintenance.[7] Prototyping fidelity can be used to mean how closely a prototype resembles the final product, ranging from low to mid to high.[8] Your approach will differ by phase.

During concept, you'll typically prototype your assumptions about the content.[9] For an exhibit about animal movement, for example, we began by testing our assumptions about appropriate words to describe how different animals move in their natural habitat. We showed children videos of real animals, then observed and noted the expressions, movements, and words the children used when viewing the animal videos.[10] Our key areas of inquiry were:

- What words do children use to describe the animals and their movements?
- How do caregivers talk to children about the animals and their movements?
- How do children move their bodies to mimic the animal movements?

Table 9.1 Prototyping plan template

Project name:
Date:
Compiled by:
Phase completion date:

Gallery	Component	Questions	Motivation/ utility	How will we test this?	What materials do we need?	Who will create the prototype?	Who will we test it with?	How will the results be shared?	Notes

Table 9.2 Prototyping terminology sample

Prototyping based on utility	Prototyping based on motivation
Looks like	To validate: test whether to advance to next step
Works like	To decide: evaluate concepts to advance or reject
Feels like	To differentiate: test prototypes for specific attributes
Sounds like	To explore: focus on behavior or response to an activity
Key questions to analyze outcomes	
• Does the element deliver the key message? • Can the visitor figure out the element?	• Will the element hold up over time? • Is the element accessible to all?

This gave us information about our intended audience in relation to the content for the exhibition and allowed us to observe and learn about this audience (in this case, children) from children themselves.

If you fully design your exhibits but wait to test anything with visitors until after installation, then you're more at risk of creating something that doesn't fulfill your intent, which will have a negative impact on quality, budget, and schedule. If you perform prototyping to prove your idea is worthy during the concept phase,[11] test various ways to solve for function and form during the schematic phase, and launch a pilot for evaluation during final design and fabrication, you're likely well on your way to creating a successful exhibit that will meet your goals and hold up to your visitors. In the big picture, prototyping will save you resources and heartache. Here are some common types of prototyping and when we typically use them:

Paper prototype: This is often done with very simple materials, such as paper, hence the name, during concept. It's essentially something in low fidelity that can be made by almost anyone on your team. It could be a hand drawing, a paper and cardboard form, or just written information taped to a wall in a specific order.

Proof of concept: This is done to prove if a specific concept is worth moving forward as envisioned. You're testing the basis of the concept and content in some type of real setting. This is generally still simple. For example, you may want to test proof of concept that children will intuitively jump from spot to spot in a "floor is lava" type exhibit, without instruction, and at what distance your intended audience can reasonably jump. You could test this concept by installing floor graphic spots in an existing children's area at different distances and record their unfacilitated interactions. In this example, you're not yet testing for mechanical functionality (how well the graphic sticks to the floor) or aesthetics (what the final design of the graphics looks like).

Functional prototype: This is often a high-fidelity prototype made by either a fabricator, designer, or builder during schematic or fabrication. This could range from a mechanical or digital interactive to graphic mock-ups or specialty lighting effects. In some cases, you may even want to build full wall sections with digital and partial mechanical elements to test how everything functions together, with different layouts, fabrication methods, and materials. Functional prototyping is performed during schematic, final design, and fabrication, gaining refinement and clarity at each phase.

Pilot product: A pilot product is something that is ready to try out in a more comprehensive way. Perhaps it's a full mock-up on an entire element that you can test with visitors for an extended period. Or it could be the component you plan to install and monitor for performance over a defined amount of time. Pilot products are often created during fabrication, construction, and installation. If you launch your exhibit with pilot products, you'll want to establish a clear timeline for testing, evaluation, and remediation.

TESTING MATERIALS AND SAFETY

Final design and fabrication are great phases to test materials and safety. We also consider this a form of prototyping, and you'll want this information to inform your final product. Material testing can be done by installing potential materials at the site for durability, testing how two different materials are joined together, or creating full-size mock-ups. For example, when exploring new material specifications for a children's exhibition, we replaced existing finishes on two walls within an existing exhibition space with the new specifications we were considering for a future exhibit. This allowed us to observe the material performance over time and make clear comparisons between traditional versus experimental approaches before making final design decisions.

For mechanical interactive exhibits, you'll want to create fully functional prototypes or pilot products whenever possible to assess not only function for the user but also safety, maintenance, and durability. The more you can test with your intended audience, the better. Sometimes even the simplest of designs that you think are tried and true can benefit from prototyping during fabrication, which will help to prevent remediation later. For example, we mocked up a simple graphic spinner in plywood, and it was extremely functional, intuitive, and easy to use. But when we performed final fabrication using a more substantial material, we found the weight of the material heavily impacted performance and could even create safety hazards we didn't see in the initial mock-up.

DOCUMENTING RESULTS

Prototyping and visibility to the prototyping process are beneficial for everyone on an exhibition project team. You should document prototypes through photos and video and designate a place to share progress and results. This can be as simple as a shared digital folder, an informal communication channel, or a written summary of prototyping results for each exhibit. No matter the mode, share progress with project teams, extended teams, and organizational leadership so that everyone can follow along. Sometimes you'll need to explain how and why the content, design, or original ideas need to shift based on what you learn through prototyping and testing. Documenting and communicating the results of prototyping will help you and your team understand this and build resilience and adaptability going from idea to design to fabrication. Through prototyping, your team will gain:

- **Experience with failure.** Perhaps something didn't work out the way you planned so you have to try a different approach or modify expectations.
- **Experience asking others for opinions or critique.** You'll see you don't have all the answers and will need to rely on the expertise of others to come up with the best solutions.
- **A willingness to try new things.** This work builds confidence to take risks on something new and rewards taking ownership of testing and tinkering.
- **Knowledge of what has been done successfully.** Building on this success will help to come up with innovative solutions that will also hold up over time.
- **Value from thinking about the long game.** By taking maintenance and durability into account for longevity, rather than focusing on flashy materials or new products that look their best only on opening day without robust testing, the product will better meet your needs in the long run.

THE MOTIVATION TO PROTOTYPE: A CASE STUDY
by Hagen Tilp

Prototyping, a fundamental stage in the design process, allows creative minds to transform design theories into tangible representations. The motivation might stem from the desire to validate content goals or to invalidate constraints, to explore various material qualities, or simply because neither idea nor design feel fully defined. Typically, the motivation to prototype is guided by intentional questions that are at the forefront of this process.

The motivation to prototype is a natural process in my design work. When the design and content have reached a point where a physical model can further inform how to advance the product, a willingness to take risks and embrace failure as a learning opportunity sets in. I find myself starting off with reviewing constraints or previously explored paths of a similar product.

In a particular case, a summer youth program had developed a model of a seagull beak. Shaped like scissors, students opened and closed it to model picking up prey. It was used to teach in a classroom setting the difficulties seagulls face when trying to pick up various-size prey with their beaks. The early prototype was tested with children for over a year, and we wanted to revisit the design to improve function, appearance, and durability.

Constraints for this creation included that the item had to fit a wide age range of children, had to be comfortable for both left- and right-handed people, and had to be durable enough to withstand multiple field trip groups each year. Additionally, multiple identical copies of the product were needed.

I found that the hinge on the original model was counterintuitive and one way to improve the functionality was to redesign the hinge mechanism. To communicate my thinking, I made a sketch and a foam core model (a paper prototype) that already incorporated the relocation of the hinge for the beak. The convincing concept and functionality around the design led me to advance to material exploration to help answer questions around durability.

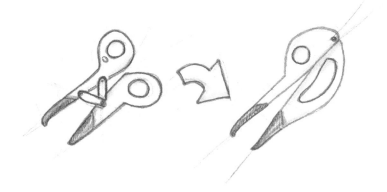

Figure 9.1 Sketches by Hagen Tilp

This signifies an important step where the power of a simple prototype can convey a direction and gain support from everyone involved.

After fabricating a wooden, functional prototype, we tested with a group of children whether this beak met our functionality goals before finalizing the aesthetics.

The modified seagull prototype was tested again, and feedback was collected. Observing the intended audience use the prototype is a significant moment. It is incredibly motivating to see it being used and will provide you with information to modify or change your design. After finalizing the design, we created a digital file for the wooden shapes and were able to create multiple copies of the final product using a laser cutter.

The described case did not require an infinite amount of iterations. While this is not always the case, it is a great example of prototyping motivated by clear intention to improve functionality and durability.

NOTES

1. Janet Petitpas, "49 Years (and Counting) of Interactivity at the Exploratorium," *Exhibition: A Journal of Exhibition Theory & Practice for Museum Professionals* 37, no. 2 (Fall 2018): 86–93, https://www.aam-us.org/wp-content/uploads/2024/03/16_Exhibition_FA18_49YearsOfInteractivityAtTheExploratorium_eb2b94.pdf. The practice of exhibit prototyping and interactivity is built on a history of innovative and exciting work by many people, including the foundational work of Frank Oppenheimer and Exploratorium staff.
2. Scott Witthoft and Stanford d.school, *This Is a Prototype? The Curious Craft of Exploring New Ideas* (Berkley, CA: Ten Speed Press, 2022), ix.
3. Paul Orselli, "Million Dollar Pencils and Duct Tape: Some Thoughts on Prototyping," *Exhibition: A Journal of Exhibition Theory & Practice for Museum Professionals* 25, no. 1 (Spring 2006): 83–85, https://www.aam-us.org/wp-content/uploads/2024/04/spring2006NAME__FULL.pdf. Orselli further describes prototyping: *"Good prototyping should be both an iterative and reductive process. If your initial ideas don't keep getting better and simpler—elegant, in both the scientific and artistic senses of that word—then something is wrong. Clever prototyping ideas never really go away, but it's important to know whether you're creating carefully crafted solutions that dovetail nicely with exhibition content, or merely making million dollar pencils."*
4. David Whitemyer, "Practice Makes Perfect: 4 Keys to Exhibit Prototyping Success," *American Alliance of Museums,* June 29, 2018, https://www.aam-us.org/2018/06/29/practice-makes-perfect/?gad_source=1&gclid=CjwKCAjwqMO0BhA8EiwAFTLgINsqC6c8jxTbr44y77ONkDZfu4OpIWJ1Ao24DwAqLgr7Du-IeBKcPhoC-MjAQAvD_BwE. Prototyping can streamline schedules through better decision-making. This takes planning, prioritizing, and support from your organizational leaders.

5. Scott Berkun, "What to Do with Ideas Once You Have Them," in *The Art of Project Management* (Sebastopol, CA: O'Reilly, 2005), 106–25.
6. Scott Witthoft and Stanford d.school, *This Is a Prototype? The Curious Craft of Exploring New Ideas* (Berkeley, CA: Ten Speed Press, 2022). Table 9.2 was adapted using a combination of terminology from *This Is a Prototype?* and framing by Hagen Tilp.
7. Caitlin Ballingall, et al., "Designing Accessible Interactives: An Inclusive Process for User Testing," *Exhibition: A Journal of Exhibition Theory & Practice for Museum Professionals* 38, no. 1 (Spring 2019): 56–66, https://www.aam-us.org/wp-content/uploads/2024/04/11_Exhibition_DesigningAccessibleInteractives.pdf.
8. Kathryn McElroy, *Prototyping for Designers: Developing the Best Digital and Physical Products* (O'Reilly Media, Inc., 2016), 39–60. This resource includes in-depth descriptions of fidelity levels (low, mid, high) with examples of both digital and physical prototyping.
9. Cathy Sigmond, "The Many Shapes of Formative Evaluation in Exhibition Development," *Exhibition: A Journal of Exhibition Theory & Practice for Museum Professionals* 38, no. 1 (Spring 2019): 34–41, https://www.aam-us.org/wp-content/uploads/2024/04/09_Exhibition_TheManyShapesofFormativeEvalution.pdf; Randi Korn, *Intentional Practice for Museums: A Guide for Maximizing Impact* (Lanham, MD: Rowman & Littlefield, 2018), 80–82. This is also referred to as front-end evaluation or formative evaluation.
10. This front-end evaluation was designed and implemented by Kristy Markowitz, Eric Nardone, and Anna Simmons.
11. Adrian Kingston, "Audience-Centered Product Development: Establishing a Digital Product Development Framework at Te Papa," Museums and the Web 2017, accessed October 18, 2024, https://mw17.mwconf.org/paper/audience-centred-product-development-establishing-a-digital-product-development-framework-at-te-papa/index.html. The Te Papa museum published a case study applying Lean, Agile, and Design Thinking methodologies with a user-centered approach to designing digital products and platforms. They allocated 10% of a proposed project budget to prototype and validate solutions at the start, leading to either approval to fund the effort or to stop the project. This is another strategy of using prototyping to streamline schedules, budget, and decision-making.

10

Feedback

Feedback will help you refine creative ideas and check your assumptions before barreling ahead. Project managers are often in the seat of including the right people and managing feedback to be productive and timely. In collaborative exhibition work, feedback will typically come from many people throughout each phase. There will be work to do to interpret how feedback is incorporated or addressed within your project. This chapter discusses ways to structure feedback sessions for various deliverables and work groups that contribute to exhibition design, development, and making.

PRODUCT REVIEWS

Product reviews are sessions to share and receive feedback on work *in progress*, which can include prototypes, preliminary design drawings, planning documents, drafts of exhibit copy, rough-cut videos, graphic design options, and in-progress exhibit fabrication. We developed the idea of product reviews with these goals in mind:

- Making our work more transparent to the whole team
- Asking for open and informal feedback between team members
- Providing a robust status update with the work product in hand
- Obtaining buy-in and approval from our leadership team or advisers
- Celebrating our work together

For product reviews, we prefer to review work in situ whenever possible. Whether it's on the conference room wall, at the fabrication and maintenance shop, or on the exhibit floor, we'll go where the product is. For large or long-term projects, product reviews are most effective on a regular monthly basis with a rolling agenda. Every working group is expected to share something during each month's review, and the agenda emerges from each work group or project lead. The week before each monthly product review, send out a call for agenda items and ask what kind of review each work group needs from other team members—feedback, approval, update, or celebration. A sample agenda template for this type of review is in Table 10.1.

We've found the regular, less formal feedback structure of product reviews helps people feel more open to sharing their work, and asking for and receiving feedback. Team members become accustomed to sharing work in progress rather than waiting until everything is complete, which allows for more iterative feedback, leaving fewer surprise moments at the end of each phase.

Table 10.1 Product review agenda and notes template

Date: Time and location: Invited/attended: Goal:						
Connection prompt:						
Time	Product	Feedback	Approval	Update	Celebration	Notes
	Interpretive media work group:					
		☐	☐	☐	☐	
		☐	☐	☐	☐	
	Content work group:					
		☐	☐	☐	☐	
		☐	☐	☐	☐	
	Design work group:					
		☐	☐	☐	☐	
		☐	☐	☐	☐	

EXCITE, BUILD, CONSIDER

As you facilitate and lead feedback processes, understand that candid feedback is crucial for aligning the outcome of a project with its goals. Without facilitation and support, candid feedback can sometimes focus on the negative, feel personal, or give undo weight to the loudest or most authoritative person in the room. We've had a lot of success addressing this problem, especially in large group settings, by helping our teams give feedback in a more structured way instead of a free-for-all. There are many established feedback routines among design thinking professionals and other related disciplines. We've developed a simple structure of our own that has been successful in both education and exhibition development processes. Over time, this structure has become a routine that places value on the ideas rather than the person presenting them, encourages more participation in giving feedback, and supports the forward momentum of ideas. We call it Excite, Build, Consider (EBC).[1]

In developing this feedback structure, we wanted to generate feedback that made our staff feel valued for their ideas and work regardless of their position and experience; provided suggestions for next steps; and acknowledged what was lacking, missing, or should be changed.

The EBC framework in Table 10.2 was the result of meeting these challenges.

Table 10.2 Excite, Build, Consider (EBC) framework

	Question to the group	*Responses begin with ...*
Excite	What about this idea are you excited about?	I'm excited about ... because ...
Build	What ideas do you have to build on what was said?	You could build on this idea by ...
Consider	What do you think we should consider changing?	Have you considered ...?

With consistency, the EBC framework can contribute to an atmosphere where people are more willing to take risks and be vulnerable. In our experience, it has created a more compassionate way of communicating that has spread throughout the organization.

Here are some tips to support the integration of the EBC framework into your work:

- **Use it regularly.** Incorporate the framework into multiple stages of the exhibition-making process so that all team members become accustomed to it. Be sure to use it early in both content development and design processes before ideas have solidified.
- **Be consistent.** Be firm in the application of the specific language of the framework during feedback sessions. This helps to normalize the process of speaking about each other's work. You may need to remind participants of the sentence starters often in the beginning.
- **Go in order.** Providing feedback in the EBC order will help people remain open by starting with the excitement, then building upon, then considering. Create an expectation that creators or makers do not respond to feedback in the moment it's given but, instead, listen closely and decide how, or if, to incorporate it afterward.

In later phases of a project or at high-impact moments of design, budget, or schedule decisions, we rely on the trust built between team members to deliver direct, candid opinions and guidance based on area of expertise. While the EBC feedback structure allows for more direct feedback to also be heard and welcome among team members, it's critical that at key moments, team members can provide necessary input without becoming too concerned with how they are phrasing their feedback. EBC is another way to build this trust during early project phases so that teams gain confidence having authentic and frank communication, which is critical for later phases of your project.

FRAMING FEEDBACK BY PHASE

As you and your team generate and refine ideas, you will need to communicate with people *outside* of your primary team members, and this is often through design documents and other visual or written communication representing the creative work at each phase. We encourage you to share content and design ideas regularly for understanding, support, and approval. This might include sharing with your leadership team, peers in other departments, staff who will maintain the exhibit after installation, or outside funders and donors. Content ideas, design, visual, and other creative work should be communicated and shared at every phase. The more you do it, the more you'll begin to see the value in getting feedback on these documents and ideas early and often. We have found that if people can't share their ideas and ask for feedback, their ideas are set up to fail in this complex field of exhibitions. That doesn't mean you have to use every piece of feedback, but new eyes will be able to see the things you can't when you're too close to the creation of ideas. We highly value creativity on our teams and expect this to come from everyone. This can also make it challenging for content developers, designers, and other creative

Table 10.3 Framing feedback by phase

Phase	Feedback framing
Concept	Defer judgment, no ideas are bad ideas Excite, Build, Consider
Schematic	Provide feedback based on your area of expertise
Final design	Direct feedback from primary decision-makers and core team members
Fabrication and construction documentation	Provide written markups on drawings
Completion	Document red-line changes on drawings for as-built conditions

producers to know when to share and what to do with the feedback they receive. On the healthiest of teams, feedback is continually sought after, direct, and useful for all of our work. You can help frame the way feedback is delivered based on the phase. Strategies for this are in Table 10.3.

NOTE

1. Bonnie Benham and Joey Scott, "Excite, Build, Consider: A Structure for Open and Honest Feedback in Project Development," American Alliance of Museums, published June 16, 2021, https://www.aam-us.org/2021/06/16/excite-build-consider-a-structure-for-open-and-honest-feedback-in-project-development/.

Part 3
Finding Alignment

Exhibition projects are by nature cross-disciplinary, bringing different voices together to create something new and unique. Working across many disciplines on highly collaborative projects can be challenging when experiences and perspectives don't align or, in some cases, are in direct conflict with one another. Productive conflict can be typical and healthy on engaged collaborative teams.[1] Nonproductive conflict can be debilitating for collaborative teams but still needs to be identified and addressed. You can set the stage for team alignment through shared values and team building, which can be very subjective and nuanced. You'll also need to establish clear processes for tough decision-making, team changes, and disagreements when they arise. This section focuses on how collaborative teams can build rapport as a basis for navigating change, assessing their ideas through feasibility, defining their methods for decision-making, and identifying and solving problems.

Note

1. Robert J. Garmston and Bruce M. Wellman, *The Adaptive School: A Sourcebook for Developing Collaborative Groups* (Lanham, MD: Rowman & Littlefield, 2016), 133–49. "Productive conflict is healthy on functional teams, and without it you may sense a feeling of apathy."

11

Building Rapport to Navigate Change

Things change. That's right, no matter how well you plan, you will inevitably make some changes during the course of your project. You'll need to adjust thinking, strategy, or expectations. You can personally be very resilient, but you don't have control over how others feel or react to change. You'll need to find ways to establish a sense of stability and team rapport for projects that encounter changes over time. This will help you set the stage for eventual change rather than being stuck in a reactionary or cleanup position when change creeps in. Perhaps a staff member leaves mid-project, new staff joins, you've been asked to delay or pause, someone changes their mind on a key priority, or scope changes in significant ways. All these things can greatly affect your team and disrupt your well-laid plans. Instead of trying to control the change, here are some ways you can help your team prepare for and respond to change.

HUMMING AND BUMMING[1]

The activity works at the beginning of a project or after a major change. Give your project team sticky notes to write down what helps them feel productive (when the team is humming) and what makes them feel frustrated (when the team is bumming). Use a balance scale image to place the sticky notes along the scale (Figure 11.1). Seeing commonalities among sticky notes on either side of the scale shows how to help each other be their most productive and illuminate shared pain points among team members. We also ask participants to write some kudos about someone else and place it underneath the scale. These notes of thanks remind the team that we all play a positive role in keeping the team humming.

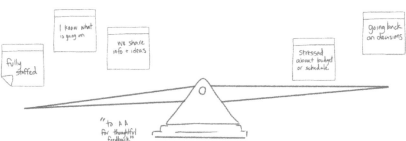

Figure 11.1 Humming and Bumming

SHARED VALUES

Group norms are a common practice in some fields to support productive communication and collaborative work.[2] Norms may include specific behaviors, such as "make space for others to speak," but a value is a deeper belief that guides a variety of behaviors, such as "we are committed to effective communication." While norms are important expectations to set up, we find that going beyond norms and into shared values can help teams build a more sustainable shared system of work. Values tend to be more abstract so it is also important to provide examples of what each value may look or sound like within a group setting.

Shared values should be created collaboratively, with involvement from your project team; extended team; leadership team; department or work group; or, even better, whole organization. It can be a significant undertaking to craft your own shared values. In the end, they can be incredibly useful in creating shared language between team members about how we commit to working together. Textbox 11.1 shows some example values.[3]

Textbox 11.1. Core value samples

We invest in healthy interpersonal relationships.
We bring a positive spirit to our work.
We are forward-thinking in our creative work.
We are committed to effective communication.
We are collaborative team members.
We bring stability to the work environment.

Sometimes we spend a lot of time crafting values, and they live pinned on the wall, rarely mentioned again. They work only if you use them authentically and consistently rather than returning to them only when there's a problem. You can include shared values in agendas and processes, calling out specific values everyone will need to lean into during different types of work. The values you emphasize for blue-sky idea generation versus giving feedback in a product review or making high-impact decisions will all be different.

PROJECT STOPS AND STARTS

Putting a project on hold is another type of change that can be disruptive, but it happens. You may already have a scale model, approved material specifications, content and research development, or design drawings. When you're in the midst of a project, you will know where all of these things are located at the tip of your finger. If you anticipate taking some time and space away from a project, you'll want to make a concerted effort to document the stopping point so that you can easily pick up where you left off. A project stop status report can capture where things are stored along with the point person for each major work product. This can also be used as team members come and go from a project. There are four key pieces of information you'll want to include in this report (Table 11.1):

- Date the project stopped
- List of work products completed or in progress (project brief, drawings, documents, models, samples, prototypes)
- Location of each work product (digital file storage or physical location)
- Point person for each work product

Be sure this report is in a common location and accessible to you and others so that it is easy to find and use in the future.

Table 11.1 Project stop report template

Project name: **Project stop date:** **Compiled by:**		
Postponed until _____, pending direction from _____.		
Last completed phase (circle one): CONCEPT SCHEMATIC FINAL DESIGN		
Work product	**Location**	**Point person**

NOTES

1. The Humming and Bumming activity was introduced to us by Lilian Asperin, AIA, LEED AP BD+C, Partner at WRNS Studio, 2023.
2. Andy Barnard and Terry Burgess, *Sociology Explained* (New York: Cambridge University Press, 1996); Robert J. Garmston and Bruce M. Wellman, *The Adaptive School: A Sourcebook for Developing Collaborative Groups* (Lanham, MD: Rowman & Littlefield, 2016). Recommended reading on the difference between norms and values and their importance for group development.
3. Beth Redmond-Jones, "Strengthening Our Core: How Defining Shared Values Can Revitalize Teams," American Alliance of Museums, published June 25, 2021, https://www.aam-us.org/2021/06/25/strengthening-our-core-how-defining-shared-values-can-revitalize-teams/.

12

Feasibility

One of the first steps to achieve alignment during exhibition making is collectively understanding the feasibility of exhibit ideas. When to deem something feasible or not is a tricky thing to gauge. Too often, decisions either come too early and have a stifling effect on creativity or so late that altering the idea causes backtracking. This ultimately impacts your schedule and budget. Many industries rely on value engineering to solve this problem, but this process can be deflating to your team and eliminate the potential benefits of pursuing high-risk or innovative ideas with confidence. Instead, we propose that feasibility discussions are continual from concept through fabrication.[1]

FEASIBILITY QUESTIONS

Understanding feasibility is more than determining if something *can* be done. Everyone on your project team has a perspective on whether something is feasible or not based on their own expertise. It's important to incorporate feedback from colleagues who work in content and design, fabrication, maintenance, facilities, project management, guest experience, interpretive media, and other related disciplines. To make informed decisions, you'll want to understand *all* those perspectives as an idea develops. You can use feasibility questions, as shown in Table 12.1, to support multidisciplinary conversations.

COLLECTIVE FEASIBILITY

You'll notice the first set of questions focus on how the exhibit idea meets content, design, accessibility standards, and other constraints. This is very intentional. If you're not meeting these goals, there is no need to proceed with the other questions. Each question should be answered by the person, or lead, with that specific expertise. For example, a content developer should

Table 12.1 Feasibility questions

Areas	Questions
How does this exhibit idea:	• meet the content messages? • meet the visitor experience goals? • meet the design intent? • meet constraints in the project brief? If not, is a variance acceptable? • impact other exhibit areas before, after, or during the project? • support universal design and accessibility standards? • meet accessibility goals outlined in our basis of design?
Materials and prototyping	• Where have we used the specified materials or equipment before? • What materials or equipment is going to be new or atypical? • Are there alternative materials, solutions, or equipment to investigate? • What materials, equipment, or function needs prototyping?
Infrastructure and installation	• What are the impacts on infrastructure, electrical, and plumbing? • What are the needs, methods and approach for installation? • Does it require floor trenching or other major alterations? • What are specific considerations to meet or exceed code requirements?
How does it affect others?	• How does it affect work already completed or planned by others? • What materials or light levels need to be reviewed by others? • How does this affect before- and after-hours events and programming?
Budget, schedule, fabrication	• How does it fit in the budget envelope? Include reasoning to support. • What in-house or out-of-house fabrication, production, or media is required? • If out-of-house, list fabricators or contractors or a need for research. • What are the schedule considerations we should take into account?
Maintenance	• Is it maintainable by our in-house teams? • What out-of-house maintenance contracts are needed for specialty items?
Risk	• What level of risk do we associate with it? High, medium, or low? • Are there safety concerns or pending safety evaluations?
Moving forward	• Can this exhibit idea move forward?

determine if the exhibit idea meets the messaging goals. An exhibit fabricator should determine what materials are new or atypical. You don't want anyone answering outside of their expertise when it comes to feasibility. So a maintenance lead isn't determining if the idea meets the design intent, and a designer isn't determining if it's maintainable by in-house staff. Take careful notes as colleagues answer the feasibility questions. Then, analyze all the answers together to determine if an idea moves forward or not.

WHEN TO ASSESS FEASIBILITY

Incorporating feasibility discussions through multiple project phases can steer you in the right direction. Aim to hold feasibility assessments three times for each exhibit component: at concept, after major changes (typically during either schematic or final design), and before fabrication. This keeps everyone informed, involved, and active in the progression of exhibit decisions. It also allows your team to change their mind given new information. When returning to a holistic conversation around feasibility is part of the process, redirections are less often seen as setbacks. Instead, the framework helps normalize iteration, agility, and progress toward ultimate solutions. The framework encourages redirection sooner than later, which also results in less value engineering and fewer surprises during fabrication and construction. You'll notice, for example, if you're struggling with the same question on all three rounds of feasibility. This process also provides motivation to take responsibility for and resolve unknowns as you identify them rather than passing them down the line to a fabricator or installer.

SUBJECTIVITY AND RISK

For a feasibility process to be successful, it's important that we acknowledge most content and design decisions are subjective. Stating this up front is critical for making sound decisions. If we pretend these decisions can be made entirely objectively, we are shutting down honesty and room for growth. You can rely on data as a basis for decision-making in many cases, but you'll have a more comprehensive assessment of feasibility if you combine data and documentation with the creative assessment, vision, and experience of your team members. For this reason, the feasibility framework invites conversation and nuance. If you base your decisions solely on one budget line item, one individual's vision, one unforeseen impact, or even visitor evaluation alone, you'll miss an opportunity to use the full knowledge base of your team and an experience to develop holistic solutions.

This holistic view of feasibility should allow your team to take risks or cut losses much earlier in your project. Identifying project risks should be encouraged so they don't remain hidden. Through feasibility discussions, as team members share ownership of how they move forward on next steps, risks can become focused, clear, well considered, and agreed upon. The knowledge and experience of team members is one of the most important factors in assessing risk.[2] This is why each discipline should speak only to their specific expertise during feasibility discussions. You'll be putting everyone, and your project, at more risk if you allow those without direct expertise to assess the risks of other disciplines.

NOTES

1. Emily Saich and Joey Scott, "REAL TALK: Assessing Feasibility with Collaborative Teams," *Exhibition: A Journal of Exhibition Theory & Practice for Museum Professionals* 40, no. 1 (season-01 2021): 40–47, https://www.aam-us.org/wp-content/uploads/2024/03/10_Exhibition_21SP_RealTalk.pdf.
2. Adam Josephs and Brad Rubenstein, *Risk Up Front: Managing Projects in a Complex World* (San Francisco, CA: Lioncrest Publishing, 2018), 222.

13

Decision-Making

Divergent thinking supports innovation, but eventually your team needs to converge on their great ideas and move them forward.[1] In a perfect world, unanimous agreements would come easily and naturally, but connecting and merging divergent ideas is easier said than done. Even teams who agree on most things will need to make some tough decisions. If you're not doing this, you're likely making passive decisions that will come back to haunt you later in the project. Make decisions out loud and clearly communicate them for shared understanding, confirmation, or even pushback. This chapter describes a variety of approaches to decision-making for collaborative exhibition teams. While we've based the approaches in this chapter on mostly traditional museum team and leadership structures, there are other models to consider for effective decision-making,[2] and you'll need to craft your processes to meet the needs of your team and organizational structure.

CONSENSUS

We use the word *consensus* to describe coming to a unanimous decision among team members. It doesn't necessarily mean everyone agrees, but it does mean that everyone can actively support the decision and will move forward willingly. It requires the full participation of everyone you're asking to decide—silence doesn't count toward consensus. Sometimes coming to consensus is easy—everyone is on the same page already, or a healthy discussion allows for everyone to get on the same page in a timely manner. Consensus works best when there is a high level of trust and communication with the group *and* when decisions are based on recommendations using data, testing, or clear advantages versus disadvantages.

DELEGATION

This strategy leans on the expertise of an individual and the trust your team has in their expertise and decision-making ability. One person is delegated as the decision-maker. For instance, if you're deciding between two different material palettes, the entire project team has transparent access to the options and the opportunity to provide feedback and input. Fabricators might speak to constructability using these materials, and content developers might speak to how the color and texture of materials support the big idea and intended audience. As the delegate, the lead designer should consider the feedback of team members while making their decision. But, ultimately, the delegate is responsible for making the final decision since their education, training, background, and job responsibilities relate to that expertise. This strategy works in a highly collaborative environment only if the team trusts the delegate, respects their expertise, and can rely on them to value the input of others.

UP TO THE TOP

You may need to involve someone from your leadership team to make decisions. Project teams don't typically love this solution to decision-making, but it might be necessary if nobody was granted the authority to make specific decisions, the team is unable to come together in consensus, or the team has a recommendation that pushes on prior constraints. High-stakes decisions should be reviewed by a leadership team for assessment of impact to the overall organization regardless. For any of these reasons, we recommend a facilitated team discussion as you bring options or solutions for approval to your leadership team. Especially in the case of high-impact decisions, you'll want each discipline to be able to speak directly to how a decision will impact their work. If you're unable to do this, you'll likely set up your leadership team to make decisions without all the essential information, which can lead to missed opportunities.

RANGE VOTING

Sometimes, when trying to reach consensus, a discussion will stall, and you can't tell where the group is leaning. Range voting allows participants to

I don't care at all.   I care a lot.

Figure 13.1 Range voting scale

better describe the nuance of their opinion. Start by stating the decision in question. For instance, you might need to decide if you're going to include a reading nook in a children's exhibition, so you'll turn this into an affirmative statement, such as *"We should include a reading nook within the exhibit space."* Provide each person with a choice of red or green sticky dot. If they agree with the statement, they'll choose a green dot. If they don't agree, they'll choose red. Then, they'll put their dot somewhere along a range of how much they care about the decision. Figure 13.1 shows this range. You'll be able to visually assess where the group is sitting with this statement. If there are a lot of red sticky dots but they don't feel strongly about it, you might ask them if they can support the idea even though they don't fully agree. If you have both green dots and red dots on the far end of *"I care a lot,"* you might have some mediation to do. You can begin by asking people to explain their position, either finding common themes or, more precisely, pinpointing where people disagree.

SWOT ANALYSIS

There are times when your team will have multiple options to pursue, or they are heavily leaning toward a high-risk option. When this happens, you'll want to make sure that people are not making quick, off-the-cuff decisions. A SWOT[3] analysis is an activity where people discuss and document strengths, weaknesses, opportunities, and threats of a particular decision. Often, we'll do a SWOT for two different options and then use the results to help ground a conversation about which one is the right choice. See Table 13.1 for an example.

For instance, a team might be deciding how to use a vacant exhibit space. Should they rent a traveling exhibit about dinosaurs or create a new performance space? Before the discussion begins, everyone involved will contribute to both SWOT charts (see Table 13.1 for an example). Then, spend time reading them and discussing commonalities and differences. Identify if any weaknesses or threats will have undo impact on your organization, or if any strengths or opportunities set one idea far above the other. The answer may not always be clear, but this will allow your team to evaluate big decisions based on shared analysis.

Every decision you make will lead you closer to the final product on any project. While big decisions can be obvious at times, even small decisions can have a ripple effect on future outcomes. Clearly identifying, as a team, how you will make decisions creates a routine of open communication and trust. Facilitating meaningful discussion around decisions will set your team on a path to supporting forward momentum and shared understanding across disciplines, even if they are not in full agreement.

Table 13.1 SWOT analysis samples

SWOT option 1: Rent a traveling exhibition about dinosaurs

Strengths
- Guests love dinosaurs—the last exhibition ranked very highly.
- Could bring in new audiences.
- In-house designers will have some design work but less than a new exhibition.
- Rental cost and shipping of exhibition are known factors.
- Fills a gap we have in our exhibition schedule.

Weaknesses
- Wasn't built for our space, so we will need to modify and add exhibit components—exhibit team needs.
- Requires marketing.
- Will need to hire additional help for install and deinstall.
- Requires enhanced security over what we currently have.

Opportunities
- Brings something new to our community that has been successful in other museums.
- We could develop exciting programming around dinosaurs (lecture with a local university professor?).
- Could be used to promote new memberships.
- Could bring in a dino movie for theater.
- Could supplement with items from our collection.

Threats
- The funding for a temporary exhibit hasn't been secured.
- It's temporary.
- Need to determine if we charge and upcharge and if that would detract from visitors' coming to see it.
- Need to determine other associated costs (install/deinstall staff, security, gallery prep, programming).

SWOT option 2: Create a new performance space

Strengths
- Community leaders have been asking for a space in the museum to use for presentation and gatherings.
- Acoustic treatment is already installed.

Weaknesses
- It may sit unused for most of the day.
- Cost to operate space has not been assessed.
- Currently, no one to manage the space, scheduling, setup, fees, and so on.

Opportunities
- We could develop exciting on-mic programming.
- We could open the space for kids' programming during the day.
- The idea is appealing for sponsors.
- Could be a space to rent for weddings.

Threats
- If we dedicate this floor space as a performance space, we might not get to use it for exhibitions in the future, as it will be hard to convert back.
- We don't currently have staff available to develop new programming.
- Community might not be willing to pay for use of space.
- Needs to be marketed properly.

NOTES

1. Sam Kaner et al., *Facilitator's Guide to Participatory Decision-Making*, third edition (San Francisco, CA: Jossey-Bass, 2014), 6-19. Recommended resource on divergent and convergent thinking, and the dynamics of group decision-making.
2. Mike Murawski, *Museums as Agents of Change: A Guide to Becoming a Changemaker* (Lanham, MD: Rowman & Littlefield, 2021), 63-80. Murawski reflects on traditional leadership hierarchy within museums and proposes collaborative and shared leadership models in Chapter 6, "Leading toward a Different Future," which can lead to more effective decision-making, innovation and growth, centering relationships, leadership capabilities at all levels, and alignment with antiracism and equity.
3. Project Management Institute, *A Guide to the Project Management Body of Knowledge (PMBOK® Guide)*, fifth edition (Newtown Square, PA: Project Management Institute, Inc., 2013), 326.

14

Problem-Solving

Sometimes project teams just hum along—everything is falling into place, and team members respect and communicate with each other. Then, suddenly, you hit a roadblock or an issue and plans fall apart. These moments can really test your team and your own confidence as a project manager. These moments will also reveal how connected your team members really are to each other. As someone managing the project, you're in a leadership position. You'll be relied on to properly diagnose the root of issues and offer opportunities for the team to correct or address them. This is tricky, and there are several ways to approach diagnosing and solving problems. You'll want to understand the mechanics of what's going on and empower yourself and other team members to solve for the long run.

IDENTIFYING CHALLENGES

Understanding the difference between technical problems and adaptive challenges can be a useful starting point to problem-solving.[1] If the issue is easy to identify and has a quick solution that can be implemented with one action, that's typically a technical problem. For example, *not everyone can make every meeting. When people can't make it, they're confused about what took place, and meetings begin to get very repetitive.* To solve this, you might assign someone to take summary notes from each meeting that clearly outline what was discussed, what was decided, and what needs further action. Share these out soon after the meeting and briefly summarize them at the start of the next recurring meeting.

However, what if team members *feel* they are being left out of meetings? Let's say they are invited but they don't often show up and don't read the notes. People think there are key meetings happening without them, or worse, there are key meetings taking place without key team members! Or team members become worried when smaller meetings take place so that every meeting has 10 to 15 people attending and small working meetings are simply not possible. You've got an adaptive challenge on your hands, and now you have some real work to do shifting mentalities. Solutions to adaptive challenges often require people to change their ways.[2]

UNDERSTANDING CHALLENGES

To begin addressing the challenge, you'll need to understand the scale, which will help you determine who should be helping you solve the challenge. The scale of a problem comes down to both impact and urgency—start by understanding both elements.

1. How many people does this challenge most affect? If it is one or two, the solution will be very different than if it impacts the entire team or even the entire organization. Less people impacted means you can focus your efforts on understanding and supporting individuals. With more people, you may need to consider facilitating deeper discussions or workshops with groups.
2. How urgent is this challenge? You probably already have a schedule and a work plan. Does solving this challenge jump the line of priorities already set? How long can you dedicate to exploring possible solutions? Giving yourself guardrails on how long you can take to solve the problem will help you plan next steps.

FINDING SOLUTIONS TOGETHER

Once you understand the challenge at hand, you'll need to do some facilitation to find collaborative solutions. You won't necessarily solve the problem in one facilitated session; in fact, that's rarely the case. If you do, then you may be solving a technical problem rather than an adaptive challenge. With an adaptive challenge, you'll likely come out of a facilitated session with a better understanding of the challenge you're solving, if solutions can be addressed through continued facilitation, or if you need mediation.[3]

If you can stay focused on building relationships, creating shared understanding, and preserving connections, you'll help your team navigate through challenges together while maintaining respect and productivity. It's when we lose sight of these things or don't truly have these intentions in mind that we see teams fall into unhealthy internal competition, avoidance, or neglecting each other's needs.

To facilitate discussions around problem-solving, put yourself in a relatively neutral position and remain curious. State the challenge you've identified and invite team members to help define it more clearly and participate in solutions. If your team is reluctant to tackle the challenge head-on through open dialogue, you'll need to give them other ways to express themselves. Here are some examples to collaboratively define a challenge *and* find solutions:

- Use sticky notes! Invite team members to write their thoughts on a sticky note, then group similar notes together to identify commonalities.
- Use a large whiteboard and invite team members to contribute over a few days on their own; then review and group those together to identify commonalities.
- Interview work groups to gather more specific information, then compile similarities and differences to how the team is viewing the challenge.
- Interview in small multidisciplinary groups, inquiring about assumptions and expectations they each have of each other related to the challenge.

You're not going to find the right solutions if the challenges remain hidden or unspoken. You can use open-ended nondirective questions to reach more clarity and depth in understanding the challenge, such as:[4]

- Can you say more about that? What else can you tell me?
- What do you mean by . . .?
- How so?
- What matters to you about that?
- Can you give me an example?
- What are thoughts about this you haven't said out loud yet?
- Is there anything you've wanted to share but we haven't asked the right questions?

If you've built enough trust through consistent communication and follow-through, these last two questions will really get to the depths of understanding what's going on. You should be able to see commonalities or differences in how your team members view this challenge and potential solutions. If there is consensus, great! Write it down, share it out, implement, and move right along.

If you're stalled in finding a solution to a challenge, refer to some of the establishing documents you created together at the beginning of this project. How about those roles and responsibilities? Can you use those to neutralize blame shifting or power grabbing? Can you refer to an agreed-upon schedule? If all else fails, do you need to ask for support from your manager, supervisor, or project sponsor? You can tap into higher-level resources in your organization and ask for specific advice or expertise on a project—a leadership team or project sponsor should be able to help you navigate tricky challenges when needed.

Facilitating groups through complex challenges requires a lot of listening, caring, and nurturing. Set healthy boundaries for yourself. You're not responsible for everyone's emotions or actions on a collaborative team. It's important that while you intentionally navigate the sometimes complicated waters of teamwork, you don't lose sight of your own needs.

EMBRACING CHALLENGES TO FIND SOLUTIONS
by Cortez Crosby

Every project will face challenges—no matter how big or small, well planned, well managed, or well funded. Challenges may stem from external pressures or internal project colleagues. They can generate great stress and unexpectedly unearth tensions within a project team. When these situations arise, it is often difficult to know how to move forward. There is no perfect answer, but here are a few insights and recommendations gained from years of managing cultural capital projects.

Look to the Project Vision and Goals

The project vision and goals must always serve as your guiding star. Use them as anchors in times of uncertainty. When working to resolve challenges, it is important that all involved parties have a shared aspiration and a common context for the issue at hand. Use the project vision and goals as a tool to remind people of why and how you got to where you are and to evaluate proposals for how to move forward.

Communicate

Open communication is critical. This cannot be understated. The best way to resolve an issue is to address it directly. Don't avoid it, because it won't go away on its own. Instead, bring people together and resist siloed communication. But before you do that, be strategic in your communication strategy. Pre-meet with key players and decision-makers to establish clear expectations and set the table for productive discussions with the broader team. Depending on your organization, it may also be important to build a cohort of supportive leadership (board members, senior staff, etc.) who can collectively strategize to target challenges at different levels within your organization.

Embrace Other Perspectives

Having a diversity of voices is a good thing. Listen to the feedback you receive, even when it can be difficult to take in or you disagree. You may learn something that deepens your understanding of the issue or informs your approach to addressing it. At a minimum, it will broaden your perspective of where others are coming from. My mantra for processing feedback is "Assume positive intent." (I find this to be true in a vast majority of situations.) Trust that others want the same positive outcome you're trying to achieve, even when they feel like obstacles.

NOTES

1. Ronald Abadian Heifetz, Alexander Grashow, and Martin Linsky, *The Practice of Adaptive Leadership: Tools and Tactics for Changing Your Organization and the World* (Brighton, MA: Harvard Business Press, 2009).
2. Heifetz et al., *The Practice of Adaptive Leadership*, 69–87.
3. adrienne maree brown, *Holding Change: The Way of Emergent Strategy Facilitation and Mediation* (Chico, CA: AK Press, 2021), 97–98. *"Facilitation is a way of listening through and beyond the words being spoken, feeling for the current of longing underneath what can be spoken, listening through fear, listening through the scar tissue: What is possible? What is the next step towards that possibility?"* Mediation, on the other hand, *"is holding space for tension and conflict to get expressed and addressed in a dispute, process, or relationship. Mediation happens when a pair or group of people cannot reach a resolution between themselves and seek the support of a third party who is relatively neutral."*
4. Sam Kaner et al., *Facilitator's Guide to Participatory Decision-Making*, third edition (San Francisco, CA: Jossey-Bass, 2014).

Part 4
Making It Real

The magic of making exhibitions is seeing ideas become reality, all the way from content development and idea generation through construction and installation. It's unlikely you'll have *all* the resources you need for an exhibition in-house at your organization from beginning to end. An essential responsibility for managing exhibition work will be selecting contractors and supporting their work with clarity and consistent communication through design, fabrication, installation, and beyond. When you select contractors and partners, you should do so well enough that you become a champion for them and they, in turn, become a champion for you. The tools and strategies in this section can be applied to contractors during all phases of exhibition making, project team members, and internal and external staff. And at the completion of an exhibition, they will *all* benefit from a thorough project closeout, reflection on lessons learned, and appreciation of a job well done.

15

Engaging Exhibit Contractors

At some point during an exhibition project, you'll likely hire services or contractors outside of your organization. This can range from content and media developers, designers and architects, to fabricators and general construction contractors. You may even need to request services from other departments within your organization. In our experience, projects with contractors and services go north or south depending on the relationship you've built with them. Treat contractors and service providers as partners with their own expertise (this is why you hired them), with respect (the same that you expect and want in return), and with purpose (otherwise you would be doing this work yourself).

CONTRACTORS, SUBCONTRACTORS, AND VENDORS

Contractors typically provide specialty work that includes materials, parts, and labor in order to make a final product. For exhibitions, this can include both consulting and design contractors, such as architects, evaluation firms, and design firms as well as general construction contractors, exhibit fabricators and other specialty fabricators, photographers, videographers, and multimedia producers.

Subcontractors are contractors that provide services within a larger project and don't contract with you directly. For example, you may select a general contractor who holds the primary contract with you (you pay them directly), and they hold contracts with a fabrication firm, an electrician, or a casework manufacturer. Importantly, you'll want your prime contractor to carry over any terms you have set to their subcontractors, such as payment terms, social media and licensing, warranties, and insurance requirements. You'll also want to hold your prime contractor accountable for establishing positive relationships with subcontractors to make sure you have optimal delivery throughout the project. If you have specialty or artistic vendors as a subcontractor to your main contractor, you will want to engage directly with them to provide artistic direction, feedback, shop visits, and clear communication.

Vendors and suppliers typically provide a known product that you use over and over, such as plywood, hardware, monitors and standard technology, graphic mounts, stanchions, or railing.

BUILDING TRUST

Building solid relationships with your contractor as a part of your team requires building trust through transparency and collaborative problem-solving, just as you would with your own team. It also requires holding both yourselves and your contractors accountable to producing and delivering work to each other so that you can both succeed. Here are some fundamental ways to build a foundation of trust from the start of these relationships:

- **Give them all the information.** That's right, ALL the information. Share your goals, the origin of your ideas, and even your budget. Think of it this way—what is the information you expect to have to do your job well? Provide your contractors with the same type of information.
- **Involve them in your team-building process.** Involve your contractor in light facilitated team building, project kickoffs, or idea generation and refinement. Finding commonalities and involving contractors in your process can establish positive communication early in a project. Or you might simply meet for morning coffee on the job site before work gets started for the day.
- **Ask curious questions.** Be curious about what your contractor knows, who they are, their expertise, and why they might be recommending solutions. Specialty fabricators, producers, builders, and general construction trades are often the final step to completing your project. While your contractor should be accountable to budgets, schedules, and work products, you, as the owner, are also accountable to asking and understanding how long things take and incorporating that into your schedule. If you have a compressed timeline, ask what can be produced within that schedule and recognize you may need to modify your expectations. Ask how things are made, ask what information they need from you, ask what you can do to help with efficiency, ask for alternatives. You want your contractors to succeed. Ask them curious questions and get the real answers, not just the answers you want to hear.
- **When in doubt, lean into candor rather than avoiding conflict.** If something isn't working for you or your team, be clear and up front about it. This is much easier to do if you've already given them all the information, gotten to know each other through team building, and asked curious questions. In any case, don't delay providing them with important feedback, what

they need to change, or providing the information they need to meet your expectations.
- **Step back from immediacy and perfection.** You want results. You want it done well. You want everyone to shine. High quality exists, quick responses exist, but immediacy and perfection will set you up for failure. We like to stay in a zone of work with contractors that connects ambition with reality. Set your ambitions. Set them high, and at the same time, understand and have honest, frequent conversations about what is realistic.

FLEXIBILITY FROM DESIGN TO FABRICATION

All contractors, fabricators, and construction trades are made of people creating real things. As with any contractor, you want to understand who they are and their capabilities. Every designer, contractor, producer, and fabricator will have their strengths and weaknesses. Establish a clear understanding of what they are especially good at and where your team is able to trust their expertise and value their input. It is equally important to know where you're stretching their knowledge or expertise. Lean into this by asking questions about their process and methods and expect to have repeated interactions to get the product you need.

Open-mindedness to the expertise of others could make a positive impact in ways you didn't expect. For example, your fabricator may have a material recommendation that not only meets your design intent but also fits better into your budget and schedule, is more sustainable, or is more maintainable. Value this input. Know where you need it and where you're unwilling to revisit your initial ideas and specifications.

Make time in your schedule to allow for feedback, communication, and input from your builders, makers, and fabricators. Allow time to test and prototype, offer alternative solutions, and recommend changes. Your project team should seek out this feedback and be open to how it might impact content and design. By listening to this feedback early on, you can avoid charging forward with a design or fabrication method that is clearly not working.

FROM, YOUR GENERAL CONTRACTOR
by Shelley Neidernhofer

As a project manager for a general contractor who works on museum and public projects, we always try to work with everyone as best we can for everyone's success. From our lens, there are a few things that can help foster a strong client/contractor relationship.

The best clients:

- Are clear about what they want and can express what they are unsure of so we can help. This is true about the scope, schedule, quality, budget, and how they want to work together.
- Are interested in a relationship.
- Respond in a timely fashion to provide the contractor with all the information they need to do their best work.
- Are easy to work with. (Not in the sense of letting us slide but, rather, are collaborative and willing to work with us to solve tough situations.)
- Trust us to help them with the services we provide (design/construction).
- Are willing to pay for services.
- Are appreciative of the services/work performed.

Contractors are also responsible for supporting the development of long-lasting relationships. A good contractor will:

- Establish trust by doing what they say they will do, performing quality work, and being honest.
- Be helpful to the client in all that they do rather than be a hindrance.
- Be respectful.
- Maintain open, transparent, and respectful communication.
- Collaborate.
- Be open-minded.
- Be flexible and nimble to changing requirements.
- Anticipate the client's needs.
- Share knowledge and expertise.
- Be problem solvers.

If contractors are part of your team, it's likely they are just as excited about your project as you are. You can support this by establishing two-way expectations and sharing the joy in seeing it all come together!

16

Developing Scope for Contractors

To acquire the services you need for your exhibition, you'll need to develop a clear scope of work. Scope is the work required to deliver a project, which includes products, services, and results.[1] While you may have developed the overall scope for your entire project within your project brief, you'll also be developing a discrete scope of work for each discipline, specialty fabricator, or maker. This chapter covers the basics of scope, samples related to exhibition making, planning shop visits, and understanding change orders.

DEFINING YOUR NEEDS

Often, the services you'll need to create exhibitions require niche trades, or specialty work. Customize the scope to be precisely the services and work that you need for your specific project and reflect the way you expect to work together.

Not only is the scope imperative for the firms and contractors you're trying to hire, writing it is also a valuable exercise that will ensure your team is on the same page about what you actually want. Core team members or on-site collaborators should be involved in writing and reviewing scope to develop a shared understanding of what to expect.

A scope of work will generally include:

- Background information
- Required deliverables
- Required documentation
- Number of revisions to account for in pricing
- Number of meetings
- Milestones and schedule
- Other expectations specific to your project

While many of your staff may be involved in fabrication, it is helpful to have one point person from your team for all primary communication with each specialty fabricator. The point person is also responsible for making sure any questions, changes, or approvals get to the right team member at a pace that is supporting the overall schedule for that work. Even as a point person, you still need to coordinate and collaborate with other team members and designated approvers. To do this, it's helpful to keep track of decisions and outstanding information needed to complete fabrication.

SAMPLE SCOPES

While scope will be specific to your project, we've included some samples for reference. Your scope may be exponentially more complex or very concise and simple. In either case, the more detail and clarity you can provide, the better responses you'll receive. The goal is to establish clear expectations for you as the client *and* for the contractor so that everyone can do their best work. In the samples provided in Textboxes 16.1 and 16.2, you (the owner, manager, museum, organization) are the client.

Textbox 16.1. Scope for photo research services

Description of work

Client is seeking the services of a professional photo researcher to identify photo sources, negotiate rights, and acquire approximately 25 final images for an upcoming exhibition on the ecology of the Maluti Mountains slated to open [date].

Deliverables

- Research photo sources for the following key species:

• *Gyps coprotheres*	• *Craterocapsa tarsodes*
• *Gypaetus barbatus*	• *Felicia uliginosa*
• *Pseudobarbus quathlambae*	• *Rhodohypoxis rubella*
• *Chlorocebus pygerythrus*	

- Provide three to five low-resolution choices per species for client review and selection.
- Acquire selected high-resolution digital images.
- Negotiate permission rights and fees for a five-year exhibition.
- Provide photo credits and captions as needed.

Meetings

- Approximately 10 hours of meetings, including a kickoff, meeting to review options, meeting to confirm choices, meeting to understand terms and fees.

Schedule

- Three months: Delivery and review of low-res images for review and selection.
- One month: Provision and delivery of high-res images.

Textbox 16.2. Sample scope for a scenic rockwork fabricator

Background

A new 5,000-square-foot exhibition about hydrothermal vents is being constructed for a large museum that sees roughly 1 million visitors per year, most of whom are families with children and general audiences. Scenic rockwork is expected in four different areas of the exhibition: the entry, gallery one, gallery three, and exit gallery, as identified in the [attached] floor plan. Content provided by client [see attached concept document with reference images].

Deliverables required

1. Maquette of each section of rockwork at one inch = one foot scale
2. Physical finish 12" x 12" sample representing colors and finish to be approved by client before fabrication
3. Fabrication of rockwork for each gallery [see attached drawings]
4. Packing, crating, shipping to the site
5. Installation on-site within specified installation schedule
6. Cleanup of installation process

Documentation required

- Consistent communication and progress photos during fabrication

Revisions

- Client ability to make revisions during shop visits

Developing Scope for Contractors

Meetings

- Weekly virtual meetings to review content and design progress
- Midpoint review in shop (either in person or virtually)
- In-person approval at fabricator shop before shipping

Milestones and schedule

- May - Kickoff and design
- July - Macquettes and review
- Sept - Samples review
- Nov - Begin Fabrication
- April - Installation

All rockwork must:

- be durable, touchable, and safe for visitors of all ages
- be able to be maintained by our in-house production and maintenance team
- be fabricated off-site
- meet floor-loading requirements

SHOP VISITS

In exhibition making, you'll often need to engage specialty fabricators and producers to create custom mechanical interactives, digital and multimedia components, detailed models, interpretive signage, scenic elements, cabinetry and casework, and more. These types of exhibits and components are most often made in specialty shops. You'll get the best product if you plan visits to their shops during fabrication and before completion and shipping to site.

When planning to make visits to specialty shops to view work in progress, consider who you might need in addition to the point person. Do you need a curator, designer, content specialist, or lead fabricator or maintainer from your organization to see and approve the work as it's getting made? Schedule shop visits at critical milestones and decision-making points before the fabrication is complete. As an example, in Table 16.1 is a schedule for in-person meetings, both shop visits and at the project site, when engaging a scenic fabricator.

In-person meetings are more feasible if your fabricators and contractors are local to your project. If that's not possible, you may need to choose which of these reviews must be in person, how many people you send, and which ones can be virtual instead. We've been able to accomplish similar reviews through virtual means, but we recommend at least one in-person meeting at

Table 16.1 In-person schedule for specialty fabrication sample

Meeting	Purpose	Location
Project start, prior to fabrication	Review design intent and content goals, and take site measurements	Project Site
Scale model review	Review model and make changes directly with artisans	Fabricator Shop
Scale model review	Ship model to project site for review by larger group	Project Site
50% fabrication review	Review fabrication massing	Fabricator Shop
75% fabrication review	Provide art direction and respond to questions from artisans	Fabricator Shop
95% fabrication review	Review fabrication before shipping to site and final art direction	Fabricator Shop
100% fabrication review	Review installation	Project Site

the fabricator shop ahead of shipping to the site for installation. This will allow you to answer final questions and give both you and the fabricator assurance that what is shipping to the site meets your expectations. If your contractor is a multimedia producer and is creating a digital interactive, the same principles apply. It's important to see how a multimedia interactive works in physical space. Create time in your schedule to make a shop visit and test it in person on the hardware you expect to use for the final product whenever possible.

CHANGE ORDERS

Change orders are changes that will cost you money. Some of these are unavoidable, and some will come from scope that you add to the project intentionally. Change orders can be caused by a gap in scope, a schedule delay, or design changes. The change orders you really want to avoid are because you didn't make your expectations clear. These will not only cost you time and money, but they can also sour relationships. They can even set you up to cut other aspects of your project to accommodate the change orders. The best way to avoid these types of change orders is to be thorough and precise with your scope. In any case, billing rates and markups for how change orders will be valued should be included in your contract terms.

If you're writing scope for contractors who are expected to either follow precedents or fabricate something, include exhibit summaries, reference images, sketches, and detailed drawings. Include all the information you would need to understand how to deliver this work. Don't make any assumptions

Table 16.2 Information matrix template

Project name: Date: Compiled by:						
✓	Item description	Requested by	Date requested	Assigned to	Deadline	Date completed	Notes

about what they might already know about your needs. If you expect to see samples or to have extended time to provide feedback, make that known. If you have specific installation, insurance, union labor, or wage requirements for your project site, make that clear. Your expectations about communication, such as a weekly meeting, or visits to and from their office to yours, should also be clear. All of these details will help colleagues, firms, contractors, and consultants understand what you expect, and they'll be able to respond accordingly.

In any process with a contractor, or even working internally with other departments, you should allow time for questions and clarification of the scope. Take the time to make sure your description of scope is well understood, that each item can be achieved, and that you align any expectations that are unrealistic or unclear before you move forward with selecting contractors.

Changes caused by missing information or indecision can lead to schedule delays, overtime, additional management fees, or redoing work. A simple tool called an information matrix, shown in Table 16.2, can help you identify and track the information contractors need to do their work. This will allow you to see, in advance, where you are at risk of causing a change or delay and prevent it (or at least not be surprised by it).

NOTE

1. Project Management Institute, *A Guide to the Project Management Body of Knowledge (PMBOK® Guide), Seventh Edition, and the Standard for Project Management (ENGLISH)* (Project Management Institute, 2013), 84.

17

Selecting Contractors

Choosing the right architect, exhibit designer, or specialty fabricator is incredibly important in making your exhibition project come to fruition. Requests for Qualifications (RFQs) and Requests for Proposals (RFPs) are common tools used to help you assess and select the right contractors for your project.[1] We've found that including some key questions about collaboration and values will help you understand and assess relationships during the RFQ and RFP process in addition to evaluating technical ability, capacity, budget, and schedule. This will be especially critical if you're expecting high levels of collaboration between your contractors and your internal project team.[2]

REQUEST FOR QUALIFICATIONS

An RFQ establishes the requirements needed to *qualify* for responding to a forthcoming formal proposal or bid. This will often pre-qualify candidates, allowing them to express interest alongside demonstrating their general qualifications, so that you can narrow down who receives and responds to the more detailed RFP. It provides contractors with information they need to decide if they want to pursue work with you before they spend the time, effort, and expense of responding to a detailed RFP. You can also disqualify candidates that clearly don't meet your needs.

You'll want input and collaboration from other project team members to ensure you've captured their expectations at the very start of this process. First, clearly introduce your organization and your project, describe the scope of work needed, and list specifically what you expect from their response. Typical sections in an RFQ are shown below:

1. Introduction to your organization and team
2. Project description

3. Schedule
4. General scope statement
5. A list of the respondent requirements
   a. Cover letter
   b. Company overview
   c. Capabilities
   d. Staff experience
   e. Relevant projects
   f. Nondisclosure, legal issues, and conflict of interest statements
6. Directions and timeline for how to respond to the RFQ
7. Your selection process

Relevant projects, in particular, are a key aspect to evaluating RFQ responses. This will show you capabilities and experience, and provide you with a former client reference who can speak about their experience working with this contractor. When you ask firms to share relevant projects during an RFQ process, clarify which types of projects will help you better understand their work in relation to your project. Following is an example:

- *Share three (3) projects demonstrating your experience and expertise providing conceptual design services through construction documents on a museum project within an open and active facility. Complex projects that include managing large teams, completed within the last five years, are preferred. Limit each project description to one page. Photos can be included as additional pages.*

You'll also want to be clear about the information you need them to provide about each reference project so you can evaluate responses side by side. The following example shows a common list:

- Project title
- Brief project overview
- Contract type
- Team members involved and a brief description of their roles
- List of collaborating firms or project partners and their roles if applicable
- Location and square footage
- Initial budget and cost at completion
- Architectural fees
- Start and completion date
- Duration of construction
- Unique features and/or construction techniques used on the project
- Contact for reference
- Photographs with captions

When you receive written responses, you'll need to decide which firms move to the next step. You may decide to offer a site visit or to conduct interviews during the RFQ process to narrow your candidates. At the end of the RFQ process, you'll form a short list of contractors who will receive your RFP.

REQUEST FOR PROPOSALS

An RFP establishes the detailed scope, schedule, contract type, and bidding process of your project so that you can select and award the project to one contractor or a team of contractors and subcontractors. The short list from your RFQ process includes the firms that will receive your RFP. At this point, they should be fully qualified and prepared to respond appropriately. We recommend limiting your short list to two to three potential candidates, but this will depend on the size of your project and the requirements of your organization.

You'll also want to identify your project delivery model in the RFP, which is directly related to your contract type. Here are three common project delivery models:[3]

1. **Design-bid-build:** This is a traditional system where the owner hires a designer or architect to design the exhibition through construction documentation. These documents are sent out to bid, and then a contractor is selected based on bidding.
2. **Design-build:** In this more integrated system, the owner hires a designer and builder to work together as a single entity. Some firms will provide both services, or firms will partner together. This delivery method has many efficiencies for exhibition projects, such as having both the designer *and* fabricator at the table during the design process.
3. **Multiple prime contractors:** This is when the owner acts as the prime contractor and hires their own subcontractors, managing the work of several contractors directly. This is common on smaller projects but can be quite complex and inefficient on larger projects.

Exhibition projects are unique, often requiring specialty services. You can and should be selective about who receives an RFP. Don't ask for RFP responses from firms you're not willing to work with. If you're clear, thorough, and thoughtful in describing your needs through an RFP process, you can expect clear, thorough, and thoughtful responses that meet your needs. But these more specific responses will take time for a respondent to complete well, so be as generous as you can when setting the timeline for when proposals are due.

If you have already performed an RFQ process, that means you'll already have their capabilities, sample projects, and basic qualification information and you won't need to ask for that again. Additional information you will provide and ask for in an RFP is noted as follows:

1. Summary of your organization
2. Detailed project description
3. Detailed project schedule
4. Specific project location
5. Project documentation (floor plans, site plans, documents, drawings)
6. Detailed scope of work requirements
7. Estimating or budget spreadsheet template
8. List of deliverables or services that will be provided by your organization (and are not included in the scope of responding firms)
9. List of the respondent requirements
    a. Cover letter
    b. Key staff who will be assigned to this project
    c. Completed estimate or budget
    d. Statement of ability to meet the schedule or proposed variance
    e. Nondisclosure, legal issues, and conflict of interest statements
10. Insurance requirements
11. Contracting requirements (or sample contract)
12. Directions and timeline for how to respond to the RFQ
13. Point of contact from your organization for questions and clarifications
14. Your selection process and timeline for award

In contrast to the RFQ, firms will respond to your RFP with specific staff, cost, and ability to meet the schedule of your project scope. If you've done this well, you'll have a hard time making final selections. To ensure you're comparing apples to apples when it comes to cost, we find it best to provide a bidding worksheet for all firms to complete that has a row for each element you outlined in your scope.

In regard to your project schedule, know in advance how much flexibility you have. You might not have all the information to know if you're being realistic about the schedule for the project at this point. For this reason, we ask contractors to make a statement about their ability to meet our schedule or if they are proposing a variance to our schedule. Having these conversations up front will help to avoid unpleasant schedule surprises or changes later on.

Allow time in the RFP process for questions and clarifications. You should provide a date by which you need questions submitted and a date by which you will answer them. When you answer questions, it's best practice to send a summary of your responses to all respondents so they all have the same information.

ASKING AUTHENTIC QUESTIONS

We find it worthwhile to include questions in both the RFQ and RFP process that are nuanced and specific to collaborative relationships, goals unique to your organization, or challenges you foresee with your own project requirements. These questions will take some effort by the responding firms to be authentic and specific. Each question should begin with a statement of your expectations, then a question for their related response. These are not trick questions, so there's no need to hide your intentions behind them. As we find in almost all aspects of working with contractors, you should give them *all* the information so they can respond accordingly. Following are a few sample questions for collaborative exhibition projects:

1. It is important to our team that the design process be collaborative and that our partners be committed to meeting goals for our standards of collections, sustainability, and meeting the needs and experiences of our diverse audiences. Answer the following question in three or four paragraphs:
    a. What is most important to you in how you develop designs for a particular project or client, and how do you measure success based on this?
2. Throughout the duration of this project, our team plans to support an iterative design process. We are seeking partners who will be dedicated to testing out ideas and participating in the prototyping process. Answer the following questions in two or three paragraphs:
    a. Describe one or two examples of past projects in which iterative design or construction solutions played a role in your work process. How have these experiences influenced your approach? What recommendations would you make in relation to working iteratively in a design-build partnership?
3. Our organization is committed to accessibility and inclusion and will look to our design and fabrication partners to share expertise and best practices in universal design and accessibility. Answer the following question in two or three paragraphs:
    a. What are your top priorities in creating accessible design, and how have you used these priorities to create welcoming, people-friendly spaces within a museum or cultural project?

You can also see that we've been clear about the length of the responses we're requesting. This has two benefits: (1) the qualifications package they send you will be succinct, and (2) this showcases that you can be clear about your expectations and establish the appropriate amount of time and energy they should spend responding. Clarity about your expectations and an awareness of the effort, time, and impact on what it takes to respond will establish a positive start to your relationship with contractors. In turn, proposals should be tailored to the needs of your specific project. Respondents should demonstrate through their proposal the ability to attend to detail and interest in your project by adhering to the requirements you set forth in the RFP.

INTERVIEWING

Based on the proposal packages you receive and the size and complexity of your project, you'll want to offer an opportunity to meet with key members of the proposed respondents for a site visit, an opportunity to discuss your project, or a formal interview. In all of these, you're looking for the best match for both technical aspects and the level of collaboration you're seeking.

For a formal interview, it is important to bring a variety of people from your team to the table. Different disciplines from your project team will be able to evaluate your candidates from their own unique expertise and perspectives. This will provide you with a more holistic way of evaluating candidates and choosing the right firm. It also helps ensure your whole team is on board with making the selection. When evaluating specialty exhibit fabricators, for example, we typically include the project manager, designer, content developer, and fabrication lead in these interviews. For architectural services, we include our project manager, designer, and a facilities or maintenance representative. If these contracts are long term and high cost, we always include someone from our leadership team.

Here are some interview questions that have served us well:

- If we were to select you to work on this project, what should we know about your firm and working style that will help make this relationship successful?
- Based on what you know about this project and our team, what do you need and expect from us?
- Please have your project manager walk us through the proposed schedule that you provided in your package. What parts of the schedule do you think contain the most risk?
- What is your key ingredient for successfully delivering this project?
- When have you made a misstep or mistake as a firm, and how did you resolve it?

AWARDING CONTRACTS

Unless you're required to award to the lowest bidder, the numbers alone don't decide for you. If you've selected quality firms, vetted them, and provided the same information to all of them, the bids are most likely going to be quite competitive with each other. If one is extremely low, that might be a sign that you have a misunderstanding or that your scope was too vague, and you'll want to dig into why that is before you snap it up as the best option. Ideally, you want one firm that is the absolute best at everything, but often you'll have to choose what's most important for a successful project. You need to understand how your team prioritizes different advantages and what's going to give you the best outcome for the project.[4] Remember, once you award a project to a contractor, you should become their biggest champion, and you'll want them to be successful.

You'll also want to keep the door open to working in the future with the firms that you did not select. Value their time and expertise by respectfully sharing why they weren't selected. Show appreciation for why they qualified and what you found competitive about their response. Give them solid information, in a timely manner, as to what they could have done to meet your needs. In some cases, it might be that they weren't lacking anything but, rather, another firm was a better fit. This will provide them with information about what you're looking for in a partner so they can decide if they want to pursue future work with you as well.

Following are additional tips to building good partnerships when selecting contractors:

1. **Value what you're asking for.** If it's above and beyond, such as asking them to solve your design problems as a part of their proposal, pay for it. Or use this process to understand how they've solved similar problems on other projects rather than asking for unpaid or speculative work.
2. **Be consistent.** Ask the same questions of everyone. You can certainly design your interview questions specifically to their proposal response. But you'll want to be able to compare proposals, so be consistent with written questions.
3. **Adhere to privacy and confidentiality.** Don't share proposals with their competitors. Sometimes firms will ask what other firms did or how much they bid, but the best practice is to keep proposals confidential. You may share how you made your decision, what they could have done differently, and how they fit into the range of cost proposals you received.
4. **Be present.** Be available, respond when and how you said you would, and answer their questions to the best of your ability. If you don't have an answer, be real about it. It's to your advantage if they have as much information as possible so they know what you're trying to achieve.
5. **Be authentic and curious.** Be open and curious about who they are as a firm, what they value, and how they work, and be respectful of their time and effort.

NOTES

1. "The RFP Issue," *Exhibition: A Journal of Exhibition Theory & Practice for Museum Professionals* 26, no. 1 (Spring 2007), https://www.aam-us.org/programs/publications/exhibition-journal/spring-2007-the-rfp-issue/. The Spring 2007 issue of *Exhibition Journal* includes an extensive selection of articles, documents, samples, templates, and matrices related to RFQs; RFPs; contracts; and procurement for designers, artists, exhibits, furniture, architects, and, more specifically, museums and exhibitions.
2. Sara DeAngelis and Cathlin Bradley, "Creative Collaboration: Rethinking Planning, Design, and Fabrication Relationships," *Exhibition: A Journal of Exhibition Theory & Practice for Museum Professionals* 38, no. 1 (season-01 2019): 102–10, https://www.aam-us.org/wp-content/uploads/2024/04/15_Exhibition_CreativeCollaboration.pdf.
3. Design-Build Institute of America, *Project Delivery: A Design-Build Done Right Primer* (Washington, DC: DBIA, 2023).
4. Rebecca Snelling, *Choosing by Advantages: How to Make Sound Decisions* (BDI Publishers, 2022). Recommended reading for additional approaches to advantage-based decision-making.

18

Communication during Construction

Communication is key to successful construction management. Let's say a drawing doesn't give the builder all the information they need, there's a change on-site, or there's a missing approval needed to move forward. And all of this is happening at once! Even if you have a dedicated site supervisor, you and your team will need a consistent presence on-site.[1] This will ensure continuity of planning and design through construction and installation. If construction isn't the phase you're most familiar with, that's even more reason to be on-site as much as possible. The knowledge and expertise you'll gain from construction and installation will better inform the planning and conceptual phases of your next project. Following are key meetings and strategies to help establish effective communication on-site.

OWNER, ARCHITECT, CONTRACTOR MEETING

The Owner, Architect, Contractor[2] meeting, typically referred to as an OAC meeting, is held weekly with a focus on reviewing main priorities for the week, reviewing the schedule for the next four weeks, and identifying requests for information that require decision-making or approval to proceed. Primary participants in the meeting should be you (project manager/project owner), your design team (this could be the architect, exhibit designers, graphics designers, or multimedia designers), and builders (this could be general contractors, specialty fabrications, or other production work). You might find that it's 15 to 30 minutes during some phases and 90 minutes in other phases.

DAILY SITE HUDDLE

This meeting is about coordinating the work on-site for the day ahead. You or your primary site supervisor should lead the daily huddle. Invite leads from each discipline working on-site to state the area they are working in, their goal for the day, and if they need support from others. This will quickly tell you if there are conflicts in areas of work to resolve, if something has changed because someone is waiting on materials, or if something wasn't completed from the previous day. You'll also notice if some aspect of the construction or installation is falling behind. If goals are not being met by a specific trade, this might mean they need more resources, they don't have the information and decisions they need to succeed, or they are not performing to expectations. The daily huddle will help you redirect issues so they don't result in unforeseen delays, problems, or major change orders later.

SHOW AND TELL

Whatever it is that you're talking about, meet in front of it. Don't talk about an electrical panel in theory when you could talk about the panel in the location where it will be installed. Even if you're talking about an exhibit component that is going to arrive soon, meet at the loading dock to discuss logistics of getting it in the building or meet in the space it will be installed to discuss how it will attach to the floor. Whenever possible, meet in front of the real thing so that you have all the information and are not making assumptions and guesses about physical realities that are forming on-site.

A LIVING SCHEDULE

Post a physical copy of your construction schedule on-site, in an easily visible location. Review this schedule at one of your daily huddles each week. Encourage contractors to mark up the calendar with shifts or changes throughout the week for visibility to everyone on-site. At the end of each week, incorporate those edits back into the digital and physical versions of the construction schedule and repost as needed. This will essentially keep your schedule alive and accurate rather than being a static and out-of-date document.

REAL-TIME DRAWING SET

Similar to keeping a physical copy of the schedule on-site, you'll want a physical copy of the complete drawing set on-site. Perhaps your team is sophisticated enough to do this all digitally, and that's fine, too, but we've found that keeping a large-format physical copy on-site allows easier double-checking before and during construction for all types of work. It encourages documentation of even small changes that happen during construction. One person, most often the site supervisor or project manager, should be responsible for managing the official drawing set. They should add new and updated drawings that are issued throughout the project and work with all trades to clearly document changes (often called redlines or markups) as they happen on-site. If your team is building from outdated drawings, or you have multiple sets of drawings throughout the site, you're running the risk of something being built wrong and putting everyone at a real disadvantage.

PRIORITIZING SAFETY

You will occasionally have people on-site who feel they've done this forever and they don't need to follow a safety protocol. But the truth is that nothing is more important than prioritizing someone's safety. Nothing—not a tour for donors, not a project milestone, not even a deadline from a CEO. You need to make sure the expectation of prioritizing safety is clear to everyone on-site, is part of the project culture, and is supported by your leadership team. Your site supervisor or general construction contractor should be leading and hosting toolbox safety talks.[3] These should be attended by everyone working on-site, and proper construction attire should also be required for all (hard hats, closed-toed shoes, high visibility vests).

In addition to government and local guidelines, here are some strategies that can be used to support a safe site:

- Create project-specific safety hard-hat stickers for completing a safety orientation or toolbox safety talk. You'd be surprised how effective a project-specific sticker can be. This is a quick way to visually know if this step has been completed before allowing someone on-site.
- Keep an easily accessible stock of clean and regularly sanitized safety gear for guests and visitors who are approved to be on-site. This helps ensure everyone is dressed appropriately as they enter the site.
- Establish a clear and effective check-in process. Safety includes monitoring who comes and goes on-site. Your construction wall should be equipped with a keypad door lock to ensure that guests and others can't simply walk in, along with a sign-in sheet to track incoming and outgoing from the site. It sounds simple, but for recordkeeping and in case of emergencies, a clipboard or digital sign-in sheet is tried and true.
- Prioritize a clean site. This is where the work is happening—sawing, cutting, sanding, moving things around. It will get messy! Make regular cleanup a priority. This may include hiring a cleaning crew or adding hours for construction staff to ensure the site is swept and clear of obstructions and debris, and all materials are put away throughout the day and at the end of each task for the day. A clean site is infinitely more safe than a messy and disorganized site.

NOTES

1. "Construction Administration," AIA Professional, accessed July 12, 2024, https://content.aia.org/sites/default/files/2017-03/EPC_Construction_Admin_3B.pdf. Architects will also be involved during construction as part of construction administration (often referred to as CA). These activities include reviewing submittals and responding to requests for information from your contractors as well as supporting approvals, change orders, document control, and closeout.
2. Ross Ludwig, "Meetings Critical to Construction Project Success and Best Practices: A Case Study," San Luis Obispo: California Polytechnic State University, 2018, https://digitalcommons.calpoly.edu/cgi/viewcontent.cgi?article=1241&context=cmsp. Ross Ludwig describes OAC meetings as "arguably the single most important meetings to take place during the construction process."
3. OSHA Training, "Toolbox Talks for OSHA Safety and Health," accessed May 13, 2024, https://oshatraining.com/more-osha-training-resources/toolbox-talks-for-osha-safety-and-health/. *"Toolbox talks are an easy way for foremen and supervisors to supplement the OSHA (Occupational Safety and Health Administration) training efforts of their company or organization, and to keep safety front and center in their workers' minds. These short pre-written safety meetings are designed to heighten employee awareness of workplace hazards and OSHA regulations."*

19

On-Site Changes

Everyone is on-site—walls are being built, electrical and data are being run, specialty exhibits are arriving in crates, and your team is installing interactives and graphics. It's a well-choreographed dance. You're supporting everyone's work with good information, plans and schedules posted on the wall, and regular huddles and walk-throughs. But then you find a hidden surprise after demolition that needs repair, a variance in building dimensions, or a critical exhibit component wasn't built to exact specifications. All of this can lead to delay, frustration, and additional cost. The best thing you can do is try to avoid them, but let's be real—they're going to happen. How you react, the ways in which you have prepared and anticipated, and the planning you've done to mitigate them will reduce delay, frustration, and cost, but it may not avoid them altogether. So have a plan for how you'll handle on-site changes.

MEASURE TWICE, CUT ONCE

Measuring may be someone's job, and it should end up accurately reflected in a drawing. But sometimes the reality of an old building, a historic site, or just the accuracy of old drawings will not provide you with exacting spaces. There are two strategies that we've found especially helpful to account for this.

1. **Measurements by multiple people.** This shouldn't be too time consuming and will be much less time consuming than finding a wrong measurement later that affects the placement or orientation of big items.
2. **Physically marking out your floor plan and major elements before you build.** This is a bigger task but well worth the time. After removal or demolition of anything previously in the space, you have an opportunity to confirm site conditions and constraints before you build. You can do this with tape, chalk, or any other material to identify potential considerations and concerns before the start of construction.

For a 10,000-square-foot project, for example, we created the footprint of our primary gallery walls and major exhibit elements out of quarter-inch material. We chalked a grid on the open floor after demolition, laid down the material representing the walls, and walked the space. This allowed us to use a laser to identify any constraining ceiling elements and to walk the floor plan as a visitor would to confirm final placement of major components and visitor flow ahead of construction.

ANTICIPATE CHANGE

Change can come from new information, such as a change in design requested by you, or it can be driven by the construction side of things. Certain materials, elements, or construction methods might not come together exactly as they do on written plans. Material or hardware specifications might be unavailable at the time you need them. Or mistakes have been made that need to be corrected. Strategies we've used to get ahead of site changes include engaging with builders early in the design process, procuring and testing samples well ahead of fabrication and construction, allocating review and adjustment time within the construction schedule, and holding a construction contingency.

SCHEDULE, BUDGET, QUALITY

As things change on-site, understanding your priorities will help with decision-making. Following are some questions and strategies to help you better assess how negotiable your project schedule, budget, and quality priorities are when changes come about on a construction site.

Schedule: Is the opening date negotiable? Connect with your leadership and marketing teams to make sure you both know when schedules and opening dates will be shared with the public. Ensure everyone on the project understands schedule priorities by posting key dates on-site and allowing time to finalize your punch list well before opening dates. Understand that if something goes wrong toward the end of a construction schedule, you'll typically need to consider a change in scope or costly overtime to get the schedule back on track.

Budget: Do you have a construction contingency? A transparent contingency allows for all our teams to feel confident in recommending appropriate changes on-site. It also allows project managers to quickly approve necessary changes as they come up. If you account for this within your budget, it will not be a surprise. You'll waste less time seeking additional approvals with changes that are necessary to keep the project on track.

Quality: How good is good enough? Visitor expectations coupled with often high expectations of museum teams lead toward an emphasis on high-quality work. If you're not willing to compromise on quality but an exhibit element is not meeting expectations or is too far behind schedule for on-time delivery, you'll need to make some decisions. Create a plan for how and when to deliver this element *to meet* your quality expectations rather than accepting a faulty product. This might be delaying it for after-opening remediation or defining a testing period after opening to make adjustments and changes. Ideally, you don't need to do this because you've been able to see it way in advance and have done the work through design, prototyping, testing, and fabrication to find issues and deliver to your expected quality. In fact, we find this quite rare, but it's still best practice to be clear about your quality objectives. Don't compromise on them. Instead, have a plan for what to do if something goes wrong.

AN APPROACH TO HANDLING PROJECT CHANGES
by Joan Adamczyk

From scope creep, to personnel changes, to making new observations, projects can get a lot of changes happening, even after construction gets underway. Change isn't always a bad thing, but it is often an upset to a project flow when it happens. The thing to do as a project manager is know that there will be changes during the project, so it is best to plan for them at the start.

Following are some causes of changes to look for and how to plan to mitigate their effect on construction using the planning process:

1. **Unclear or missing information in the plan documents:** Check the document phase schedule for this. Do the architect and engineering (A/E) teams have enough time to complete their portions of the documents? Is there consensus at the start on how much detail will be included in construction documents and how to manage the flow of information if the construction starts work without some details? Some projects start with documents that are developed only enough to get a permit awarded. It's up to the team at the start to decide to develop documents further from "permit set" to "construction documents" and how complete they need to be before the construction starts.
2. **Not enough time for thorough review:** Best practices are to plan for enough time for thorough review, solid decisions, and consensus on the plans. Get approvals in written form either by an email confirmation or initials on the plan set. Quite often, changes happen because collaborators didn't have the chance to review and agree on the plan, so build in time for that.

3. **Poor communication and not enough of it during the design stage to ask and receive feedback from appropriate team members:** Effective communication strategies will be a big part of the project list of goals. It is best to develop goals to keep communication open with enough time in each stage of the project for internal reviews and external adjustments to the plans.
4. **Personnel or team dynamic changes:** Just a different point of view can cause changes at any point in a project. These can be unanticipated but how they are managed should not be. If there are changes due to team member changes, this will follow the same goals for project communication. Keep the other team members informed and engaged in the review of any changes realized during team adjustments.
5. **Lack of partner management defining who needs to be consulted at the beginning of the project with team agreement on how to engage and prioritize their input:** While creating the communication strategies at the start of the project, list everyone involved and identify their roles and responsibilities. Use of the standard RACI (responsible, accountable, consulted, informed) chart is great for this. Keep this roster up to date regularly on all project activities and engage them frequently in decision-making during the design process. They will be less likely to come back during construction to know they had a part in the design.

Changes happen in construction. This is a fact. Through thoughtful consideration in a project communication strategy and scheduling enough time for plan reviews, a project can keep those changes manageable through all of its stages.

20

Completion

Seeing the physical manifestation of everyone's work come to life in an exhibition is always gratifying. On major capital projects that span several years, you may also see fatigue setting in. You'll need to support a strong completion process that will inform future planning and projects. As you complete a project, take the time to wrap up documentation and results. Organizing and archiving project files, as well as closeout reports and documentation to inform both ongoing maintenance and future collaborations, can be a big part of this process.

PUNCHLISTING

Punchlisting is creating a list of what needs to be completed, fixed, or modified in some way prior to opening. Punchlisting ensures that what's built meets your expectations and is acceptable. We recommend starting your punchlisting process midway through construction to get ahead of any major issues and providing clear communication about each item's level of priority. If you wait until the very end of construction to begin punchlisting or don't prioritize appropriately, you might find big issues to resolve, some of which may prevent you from opening to the public.

A great place to begin generating a punch list is by referring back to your control documentation—scope, contracts, specifications, confirmation of changes already approved, and drawing documentation. Use a punch-list spreadsheet, like the example in Table 20.1, as you walk the construction site and document what's acceptable, what has an allowable variance, or what's not accepted. Take photos of punch-list items whenever possible. When paired with the written spreadsheet, photos can help clearly communicate areas or items that need to be addressed. If something's not accepted, note what needs to be repaired, modified, or completed in order to be accepted.

Table 20.1 Punchlist template

Project name: Date: Compiled by:					
Completed	Category (repair, redo, install, purchase, clean)	Item description	Location	Responsible	Notes/photos
☐					
☐					
☐					
☐					

COMMISSIONING

As you finish construction, you'll want to confirm that everything was built to your requirements and specifications, and that your on-site staff are prepared to operate and maintain any systems or exhibits. In general construction terms, this is called commissioning, and similar principles apply to exhibitions. Schedule time for fabricators and contractors to train your maintenance staff and deliver operations and maintenance manuals so that you'll be able to efficiently address any issues that arise when you take ownership. Operations and maintenance (O&M) manuals should include the following:

- Materials and finishes
- Part numbers and manufacturers
- Original equipment manufacturer (OEM) information
- Drawings
- Electrical or programming schematics
- Maintenance instructions
- Troubleshooting
- Warranty information
- Contact information

BUDGET REPORT

The goal of this report is to summarize when and how you spent the project funds. Analyze the final numbers against your projections for concept, schematic, and final design phases to inform your next conceptual budget, especially if there were any surprises or changes along the way. You'll want to compare the original budget or estimate to the actual spent by different variables, such as the following:

- Overall
- By phase
- By year
- By discipline
- For each major contract (designer, architect, construction, specialty fabricators)

This report can be used to share with your leadership team or funders and can help you begin planning and budgeting your next project. Since material and labor costs are always changing, understand that recent examples will be able to inform but not determine future budgets. All analysis of budget and spending will better inform your ability to manage each ensuing project. For smaller projects, you may want to track just variance between estimated and actual costs.

SCHEDULE REPORT

A schedule report summarizes the planned versus actual duration of phases and major activities, and the reason for any variance between them. In some cases, your team will be humming along, and you'll find yourself ahead of schedule. You'll still want to analyze your schedule to understand any areas where you fell behind and why. Perhaps there was an impact from last-minute on-site changes or a gap in scope, capabilities, or resources. Whatever the reason, seek to understand so you can account for this on future projects. This report can be humbling if you were also the one who guided the team in creating the schedule in the first place. It's important to analyze your schedule without feeling defensive. Instead, try to construct this report with a sense of curiosity that will drive lessons learned. Sections of a schedule report will include the following:

- Activity (demolition, wall construction, painting, graphic installation, etc.)
- Estimated duration
- Actual duration
- Variance explanation

REMEDIATION REPORT

Change after opening is called remediation. This is common in exhibitions and other creative fields producing novel and unique components. These components often require extended periods of field testing with the public to truly identify vulnerabilities or breaking points. These longer-term items go on your remediation report along with anything that comes out of your summative evaluation.[1] With complex mechanical, electromechanical, or digital components, we recommend a 30-day post-opening and a 90-day post-opening review to create your remediation list. That way you can look at all the items as a whole and prioritize them appropriately instead of addressing them one by one. Your remediation report should describe the following:

- What needs to change?
- Why does it need to change (not working as intended, change in design, change in fabrication method)?
- Who will make the changes?
- When will the changes be made by?
- How will the changes be reviewed and approved?

RETROSPECTIVES

Structured reflections or retrospectives support an iterative, positive work team. Different strategies for looking back on the project are going to work for different groups. One constant that we've found to be most successful is focusing on how process, product, and relationships are *all* contributing factors on a project. A lot of reflections will focus just on the product, but we've found that also focusing on how the team worked together can illuminate lessons learned and opportunities for growth. Based on the data from your budget, schedule, and remediation reports, you should be able to craft retrospective questions specific to your project. The more intentional you are with the questions you ask, the better information you will gather. Here are some example retrospective questions:

- What is something you did on this project that you're proud of?
- What did someone else do that made this project better?
- What was a process or routine that helped you do your work well?
- What roles, tools, processes, or routines should we consider revising for the next project?
- What is something you could have done to make this project better?

Include both internal project staff, external contractors and collaborators, and members of your leadership team in reflection workshops. This is important to help people better understand the impact their work and actions have on others. On smaller projects, you might be able to do this as one group. On larger projects, with too many players to reflect together, it's helpful to host retrospectives by discipline and share overall results as a summary of lessons learned.

Sometimes you need a neutral facilitator to lead retrospectives. If your first attempt turns negative or awkward, or you feel defensive, that could be an indication that you need a neutral facilitator to run this for you. You also might ask an outside person to facilitate if you anticipate that stories or issues are going to be wildly different from person to person. In this case, a facilitator from outside of the project can help to establish a baseline of truth or, at least, facilitate from a more neutral position. If you don't have a neutral facilitator to lean on, one-on-one sessions are usually the way to go. This allows people to share honest critique and feedback in a lower-stakes environment.

It's essential to take thorough notes and share common themes or outliers as a result of the retrospectives. Ideas or issues that come up multiple times should be shared for transparency and accountability to the project team. If something is mentioned by multiple people, you should advocate for addressing it. Feedback from retrospectives can have implications on how you staff the next project, how you allocate time and resources, and your approach to future hiring practices with your contractors.

NOTE

1. Randi Korn, *Intentional Practice for Museums: A Guide for Maximizing Impact* (Lanham, MD: Rowman & Littlefield, 2018), 82. *"Summative evaluation is conducted after installation or implementation and examines the overall effectiveness of a project on audiences."*

21

Celebrating the Work

You can help your team celebrate their amazing, complex, and important work both throughout a project and at the end of a project. Opening parties for staff, contractors, and their families are one way to celebrate the work. We also advocate for regularly appreciating each other's work, connecting to each other, and reflecting on your own and each other's contributions as ways to celebrate *throughout* a project. Establishing these habits within a team can take time, but as it builds, you'll discover how individuals express and feel gratitude[1] for each other and themselves, how they relate to each other, and what you can do to bring your team closer together as they do this complex, creative, and collaborative work.

APPRECIATING

We find that appreciation among a trusting team goes a long way in continuing positive, collaborative relationships. A sincere appreciation recognizes and acknowledges someone's contribution in a way that is truthful about the contribution, is in line with the value of that contribution, and aligns with how someone perceives themselves and their contributions on the team. Insincere appreciation, however, can detract from trust and team building. It might be something that diminishes one's contributions (a backhanded compliment) or does not align well with how they see themselves fitting into the project team in a positive way. Not everyone is accustomed to expressing appreciation or accepting appreciation.

When you think about appreciation, think about how to encourage the practice as consistent and routine in both formal and informal ways. This work begins all the way back in the concept phase of your project. If you know what's expected of someone through clear roles and responsibilities, and they perform or go above and beyond, it can be fairly simple to recognize this work.

If you don't have clear roles, and everyone is stepping all over everyone else, or worse, tiptoeing around each other, it becomes really difficult to appreciate someone without diminishing someone else.

Establishing regular places to express your appreciation lets people know where to give and where to look for appreciations, and it can be visible to the whole team for celebration. You can do this in a project team chat channel, which is useful for impromptu as well as prompted appreciation. If you're prompting appreciation, it can be helpful to encourage your team to appreciate each other based on something specific. Here are a few to try:

- Appreciate someone on the team who really exemplified one of our shared values this week.
- What did someone on the team do this week that made your work better?
- Who brought joy or inspiration into the room this week?

CONNECTING

Connection prompts[2] are thoughtful questions or sentence starters that are designed to help team members connect on a specific topic in order to center the upcoming work, promote empathy, or otherwise build working relationships. They are best used before or after product reviews and other major deliverables and can help center a team on the present moment and gain a deeper appreciation and understanding of each other and the unique place we all hold in this work. We recommend giving people a heads up on the prompt so they have some time in advance to consider whom they want to appreciate or how they want to express themselves. Some samples are in Table 21.1.

Following are a few rules of thumb on connection prompts:

- **Be genuine and authentic.** Ask questions that are meaningful and model authentic appreciation.
- **Don't dig too deep.** You are seeking authenticity, not group therapy.
- **Be timely.** Fine-tune your prompts to the moment so appreciation can be expressed regularly and about current things rather than asking people to recollect from months ago.

GIVING RECOGNITION

You can recognize work accomplished through a brag tour. Just before your opening, walk through the exhibition with the project team, inviting each person to share work they did that they are proud of. Maybe it's an especially eloquent label, a beautifully sourced photo, a tricky interactive, or the paint color on the wall. It could even be the cleanliness of the site in general, a decision or meeting that informed the final product, clearly documented redlines on the

Table 21.1 Connection prompts

Category	Questions
Appreciation of others	• What's something you have learned from someone else at this table (or on this team)? • What did someone do this week that made your work easier?
Appreciation of self	• What's something you're really proud of doing this past week? • What is something you have learned on this project?
Gratitude	• What's something your younger self did that you're grateful for today? • What's something that brought you inspiration this week?
Self-reflection	• When was the last time you changed your mind in light of new information? • What is something that went well because you did it with other people on the team? • When were you either humming or bumming this past week, and why?

drawing set, or the relationship built between designer and curator. Be sure to curb criticism on a brag tour, as this is a time for the team to celebrate the incredible work they've done with their colleagues, not to criticize or point out issues. If space and time allow, be generous with your invite list for this. A brag tour can contribute to high morale while closing out a project by acknowledging the skill and dedication it takes to do this work by the hands and minds of many people.

Taking the time to appreciate yourself, your colleagues, and your work can help to inform future planning and help you and your team sustain energy and enthusiasm for the next project.

NOTES

1. Kiersten F. Latham and Brenda Cowan, eds., *Flourishing in Museums: Towards a Positive Museology* (London: Routledge, 2024), 267-72. For additional context on gratitude in relation to museum practice. *"What determines whether an individual feels grateful or not has been linked to a variety of factors—from personality, to cognition, to gender, to evolution, to one's disposition. Each of these, in turn, can influence the role gratitude might play in how a person feels in a certain situation."*
2. Connection prompts are based on the work of Dr. Jenny de la Hoz, whose expertise includes building inclusive teams, 2020.

22

Themes and Takeaways

We hope this book has provided you with ideas, new tools and processes, and support for the complex and collaborative work of creating and making exhibitions. You might have noticed throughout this book that one of our favorite tools is the humble sticky note. In addition to using sticky notes for idea generation and creative development, writing a short takeaway on a note and sticking it to your office wall or work area is a quick and easy way to keep themes and takeaways top of mind. To conclude this book, we summarized a few themes and takeaways that you might consider adding to your workspace by sticky note. Or make your own!

THINKING BIG AND SMALL

Workplace training will sometimes differentiate between detail-oriented and big-picture thinkers. In this work, you must be both. You have to be prepared to facilitate agenda item number two in tomorrow's meeting and understand how what is happening today impacts the work 6 to 12 months down the line. You have to be able to create both detailed task lists and multiyear project plans.

Small decisions sometimes have big impacts on the visitor experience. For instance, the strength of the magnet in a spinner is a small decision in the grand scheme of exhibition making, but the wrong decision could make the experience so cumbersome that visitors don't get the main message of the interactive itself. Big decisions, such as how much floor space to allocate to your new exhibition, obviously have big impacts, but they require many small decisions to get there.

There are a million small details and decisions that go into developing, designing, and installing a new exhibition. And many of these lead to big impacts. If you felt personally responsible for all of them, you'd surely spontaneously combust. A key to your sustainability is to be able to think both big and small and remember you're part of a team.

BUILDING RESILIENCE

Sometimes processes don't work. Sometimes the great idea isn't feasible. Sometimes funding falls through. Sometimes the interactive breaks in the first week of opening. Whether it's rebuilding a team, finding someone to fix the broken thing, revising a schedule or budget, or switching up a process to get the work done on time, you have to be able to move through failure and disappointment. Know that when you're in the thick of a project and things aren't working out perfectly, you're building that confidence and resilience for the next project—because both success and failure are inevitable when you're willing to be innovative.

EMBRACING CURIOSITY

We think one of the most fun parts of working in exhibitions is that you get to create new things, push boundaries, learn, try, test, make, and more. To do this work, you have to remain curious. New projects will spur you to learn even more new content and gain exposure to new design ideas, different fabrication methods, and inventive construction solutions. Approaching all of this with curiosity will help you stay positive, effective, and engaged.

VALUING PEOPLE *AND* PRODUCTS

To make exhibitions, you'll need to work with people from many diverse disciplines. You'll need to build empathy for people with lots of different types of expertise and ways of working, such as the following:

- Content developers searching for the main message in a slew of possibilities
- Exhibit designers holding content, infrastructure, and code constraints all at once
- Exhibit fabricators and technicians building inventive things and troubleshooting interactive exhibit elements after opening
- Mount makers, conservators, and art handlers responsible for irreplaceable objects and artifacts before, during, and after the exhibition run
- Maintainers who will be cleaning, repairing, and replacing materials throughout the life span of an exhibition
- City plan checkers trying to make sure everything is safe and code compliant for the public

Spending time getting to know people's work builds your empathy and understanding. Maintain the perspective that all work is done by people, we all hold different expertise and experiences, and you can value all of it.

APPRECIATING YOURSELF

You may be the person on the team who sets others up for success, synthesizing large amounts of competing priorities and information, and being relied upon as a trusted sounding board for the work (and feelings) of others. Recognizing and appreciating your contributions to a collaborative team can help you maintain perspective and avoid burnout or apathy.

Following are ways to appreciate and nurture yourself:

- Keep a running list of accomplishments and things you're proud of throughout the project.
- Practice regular self-care and small moments through walks outside, lunch with people you enjoy spending time with, or other activities away from your desk, phone, or computer.
- Write down positive qualities you bring to the team on a sticky note and post this on your computer screen as a daily reminder of your own value.
- At the end of the week, remind yourself of the good work you've done so that you enter the weekend with positivity.

- Set helpful boundaries. While creating the best exhibit and opening on time and on budget is probably something you care deeply about, successes or failures along the way don't define you as a person. Consciously set boundaries that work for you to support your own sustainability.

In kind, we'd like to close this book with an appreciation for you, the reader, for being open to new collaborative approaches and for engaging in the inspiring and magical work of exhibition making.

Bibliography

"25th Anniversary Issue." *Exhibition: A Journal of Exhibition Theory & Practice for Museum Professionals* 25, no. 1 (Spring 2006): 71–77. https://www.name-aam.org/exhibition_spring2006.

Abramovici, Adrian. "Controlling Scope Creep." PM Network, 2000. Accessed July 12, 2024. https://www.pmi.org/learning/library/controlling-scope-creep-4614.

ADA.gov. "The Americans with Disabilities Act," May 22, 2024. https://www.ada.gov/.

AIA Professional. "Construction Administration." Accessed July 12, 2024. https://content.aia.org/sites/default/files/2017-03/EPC_Construction_Admin_3B.pdf.

American Alliance of Museums. "Sustainable Exhibition Design & Construction Toolkit." Accessed June 20, 2023. https://www.aam-us.org/2023/06/20/sustainable-exhibition-design-construction-toolkit/?gad_source=1&gclid=CjwKCAjwqMO0BhA8EiwAFTLgID8Fn2kQ3ouRFMsmLJNmPiaRQzRdguIaTQQaVa-c04ljxbXkUmdGrRoCRI8QAvD_BwE.

Anaissie, Tania, David Clifford, Susie Wise, and National Equity Project [Victor Cary and Tom Malarkey]. "Liberatory Design." Liberatory Design. Accessed July 12, 2024. https://www.liberatorydesign.com/.

Ballingall, Caitlin, Sheri Levinsky-Raskin, Barbara Johnson Stemler, and Jessica Williams. "Designing Accessible Interactives: An Inclusive Process for User Testing." *Exhibition: A Journal of Exhibition Theory & Practice for Museum Professionals* 38, no. 1 (Spring 2019): 56–66. https://www.aam-us.org/wp-content/uploads/2024/04/11_Exhibition_DesigningAccessibleInteractives.pdf.

Barnard, Andy, and Terry Burgess. *Sociology Explained*. New York: Cambridge University Press, 1996.

Benham, Bonnie, and Joey Scott. "Excite, Build, Consider: A Structure for Open and Honest Feedback in Project Development." American Alliance of Museums. Published June 16, 2021. https://www.aam-us.org/2021/06/16/excite-build-consider-a-structure-for-open-and-honest-feedback-in-project-development/.

Berkun, Scott. *The Art of Project Management*. Sebastopol, CA: O'Reilly, 2005.

Berkun, Scott. "What to Do with Ideas Once You Have Them." In *The Art of Project Management*, 106-25. Sebastopol, CA: O'Reilly, 2005.

brown, adrienne maree. *Holding Change: The Way of Emergent Strategy Facilitation and Mediation*. Chico, CA: AK Press, 2021.

Brown, Tim, and Barry Martin Katz. *Change by Design: How Design Thinking Transforms Organizations and Inspires Innovation*. New York: HarperCollins, 2019.

Bruman, Raymond, and Ron Hipschman. *Exploratorium Cookbook: A Construction Manual for Exploratorium Exhibits*. Vol. I-III. 1975. Reprint, San Francisco, CA: Exploratorium, 2005.

Canty, Denise. *Agile for Project Managers*. New York: CRC Press, 2015. https://doi.org/10.1201/b18052.

Centre for Excellence in Universal Design. "About Universal Design," accessed October 24, 2024, https://universaldesign.ie/about-universal-design.

Chicone, Sarah J., and Richard A. Kissel. *Dinosaurs and Dioramas: Creating Natural History Exhibitions*. Walnut Creek, CA: Left Coast Press, 2014.

Ciaccheri, Maria Chiara. *Museum Accessibility by Design: A Systemic Approach to Organizational Change*. Lanham, MD: Rowman & Littlefield, 2022.

Crellin, Naomi, and Lauren Telchin Katz. "Design-Thinking Approaches to Exhibition Development: Investigating New Ways of Working." *Exhibition: A Journal of Exhibition Theory & Practice for Museum Professionals* 38, no. 1 (Spring 2019). https://static1.squarespace.com/static/58fa260a725e25c4f30020f3/t/5cd2146d9b747a1f1582f15d/1557271689448/14_Exhibition_DesignThinkingApproachesToExhibitionDevelopment.pdf.

DeAngelis, Sara, and Cathlin Bradley. "Creative Collaboration: Rethinking Planning, Design, and Fabrication Relationships." *Exhibition: A Journal of Exhibition Theory & Practice for Museum Professionals* 38, no. 1 (Spring 2019). https://www.aam-us.org/wp-content/uploads/2024/04/15_Exhibition_CreativeCollaboration.pdf.

Design-Build Institute of America. *Project Delivery: A Design-Build Done Right Primer*. Washington, DC: DBIA, 2023.

Doorley, Scott, Carissa Carter, and Stanford d.school. *Assembling Tomorrow: A Guide to Designing a Thriving Future*. Berkeley, CA: Ten Speed Press, 2024.

Falk, John H. *Identity and the Museum Visitor Experience*. Walnut Creek, CA: Left Coast Press, 2009.

Garfinkle, Robert, and Susan Koch. "Project Management and Innovative Exhibitions: A Perfect Pair." In *Are We There Yet? Conversations about Best Practices in Science Exhibition Development*, 21-23. San Francisco, CA: Exploratorium, 2004.

Garmston, Robert J., and Bruce M. Wellman. *The Adaptive School: A Sourcebook for Developing Collaborative Groups*. Lanham, MD: Rowman & Littlefield, 2016.

Goel, Ashish, and Stanford d.school. *Drawing on Courage: Risks Worth Taking and Stands Worth Making*. Berkeley, CA: Ten Speed Press, 2022.

Gray, Dave. "Squiggle Birds." Gamestorming. February 27, 2015. https://gamestorming.com/squiggle-birds/.

Greenberg, Sarah Stein, and Stanford d.school. *Creative Acts for Curious People: How to Think, Create, and Lead in Unconventional Ways*. Berkeley, CA: Ten Speed Press, 2021.

Heifetz, Ronald Abadian, Alexander Grashow, and Martin Linsky. *The Practice of Adaptive Leadership: Tools and Tactics for Changing Your Organization and the World*. Brighton, MA: Harvard Business Press, 2009.

Hendrickson, Chris, Carl Haas, and Tung Au. "Cost and Schedule Control, Monitoring and Accounting." Pressbooks, March 1, 2024. https://ecampusontario.pressbooks.pub/projectmanagementforconstructionanddeconstruction/chapter/cost-and-schedule-control-monitoring-and-accounting/.

Hill, Kristin, Katherine Copeland, and Christian Pikel, eds. *Target Value Delivery: Practitioner Guidebook to Implementation*. Arlington, VA: Lean Construction Institute, 2016.

IDEO U. "What Is Brainstorming?" Accessed October 17, 2024, https://www.ideou.com/pages/brainstorming.

Joseph, Barry. *Making Dinosaurs Dance: A Toolkit for Digital Design in Museums*. Lanham, MD: Rowman & Littlefield, 2023.

Josephs, Adam, and Brad Rubenstein. *Risk Up Front: Managing Projects in a Complex World*. San Francisco, CA: Lioncrest Publishing, 2018.

Kaner, Sam, Lenny Lind, Catherine Toldi, Sarah Fisk, and Duane Berger. *Facilitator's Guide to Participatory Decision-Making*. Third Edition. San Francisco, CA: Jossey-Bass, 2014.

Kelley, Thomas, and David Kelley. *Creative Confidence: Unleashing the Creative Potential within Us All*. New York: Crown Publishing Group, 2013.

Klein, Katherine. "Is Your Team Too Big? Too Small? What's the Right Number?" Knowledge at Wharton, June 14, 2006. https://knowledge.wharton.upenn.edu/podcast/knowledge-at-wharton-podcast/is-your-team-too-big-too-small-whats-the-right-number-2/.

Knapp, Jake, John Zeratsky, and Braden Kowitz. *Sprint: How to Solve Big Problems and Test New Ideas in Just Five Days*. New York: Simon & Schuster, 2016.

Korn, Randi. *Intentional Practice for Museums: A Guide for Maximizing Impact*. Lanham, MD: Rowman & Littlefield, 2018.

Latham, Kiersten F., and Brenda Cowan, eds. *Flourishing in Museums: Towards a Positive Museology*. London: Routledge, 2024.

Lord, Barry, Gail Dexter Lord, and Lindsay Martin. *Manual of Museum Planning: Sustainable Space, Facilities, and Operations*. Third Edition. Lanham, MD: AltaMira Press, 2012.

Ludwig, Ross. "Meetings Critical to Construction Project Success and Best Practices: A Case Study." San Luis Obispo: California Polytechnic State University, 2018. https://digitalcommons.calpoly.edu/cgi/viewcontent.cgi?article=1241&context=cmsp.

Lupton, Ellen. *Design Is Storytelling*. Washington, DC: Cooper Hewitt, 2017.

McElroy, Kathryn. *Prototyping for Designers: Developing the Best Digital and Physical Products*. O'Reilly Media, Inc., 2016.

McKenna-Cress, Polly, and Janet A. Kamien. *Creating Exhibitions: Collaboration in the Planning, Development, and Design of Innovative Experiences.* Hoboken, NJ: John Wiley & Sons, Inc., 2013.

McLean, Kathleen. *Planning for People in Museum Exhibitions.* Washington, DC: Association of Science and Technology Centers, 1993.

McLean, Kathleen, and Catherine McEver, eds. *Are We There Yet?: Conversations About Best Practices in Science Exhibition Development.* San Francisco, CA: Exploratorium, 2004.

Morris, Martha. *Managing People and Projects in Museums: Strategies That Work.* Rowman & Littlefield, 2017.

Murawski, Mike. *Museums as Agents of Change: A Guide to Becoming a Changemaker.* Lanham, MD: Rowman & Littlefield, 2021.

MuseumNext. "Inspiring Online Learning for Museum Professionals," July 2, 2024. https://www.museumnext.com/.

Museums and the Web 2017. "Audience-centered Product Development: Establishing a Digital Product Development Framework at Te Papa," April 2017. https://mw17.mwconf.org/paper/audience-centred-product-development-establishing-a-digital-product-development-framework-at-te-papa/index.html.

Nicolaïdes, Kimon. *The Natural Way to Draw: A Working Plan for Art Study.* Houghton Mifflin, 1941.

Norris, Linda, and Rainey Tisdale. *Creativity in Museum Practice.* Walnut Creek, CA: Left Coast Press, 2014.

Olesund, Erik, Sarah Stein Greenberg, Carissa Carter, and Paul Rothstein. "High Fidelity, Low Resolution." In *Creative Acts for Curious People: How to Think, Create, and Lead in Unconventional Ways,* 202–5. Berkeley, CA: Ten Speed Press, 2021.

Olinsky, Elissa. "Maslow in Museums." Accessed October 17, 2024. https://www.frankleolinsky.com/maslow-in-museums.

Orselli, Paul. "Million Dollar Pencils and Duct Tape: Some Thoughts on Prototyping." *Exhibition: A Journal of Exhibition Theory & Practice for Museum Professionals* 25, no. 1 (Spring 2006): 83–85. https://www.aam-us.org/wp-content/uploads/2024/04/spring2006NAME__FULL.pdf.

OSHA Training. "Toolbox Talks for OSHA Safety and Health." Accessed May 13, 2024. https://oshatraining.com/more-osha-training-resources/toolbox-talks-for-osha-safety-and-health/.

Pervaiz, Sabeeh, Guohao Li, and Qi He. "The Mechanism of Goal-Setting Participation's Impact on Employees' Proactive Behavior, Moderated Mediation Role of Power Distance." *PLoS One* 16, no. 12 (December 15, 2021): e0260625. https://doi.org/10.1371/journal.pone.0260625.

Petitpas, Janet. "49 Years (and Counting) of Interactivity at the Exploratorium." *Exhibition: A Journal of Exhibition Theory & Practice for Museum Professionals* 37, no. 2 (Fall 2018): 86–93. https://www.aam-us.org/wp-content/uploads/2024/03/16_Exhibition_FA18_49YearsOfInteractivityAtTheExploratorium_eb2b94.pdf.

Piacente, Maria. *Manual of Museum Exhibitions*. Lanham, MD: Rowman & Littlefield, 2022.

Pressman, Heather, and Danielle Schulz. *The Art of Access: A Practical Guide for Museum Accessibility*. Rowman & Littlefield, 2021.

Project Management Institute. *A Guide to the Project Management Body of Knowledge (PMBOK® Guide)*. Fifth Edition. Newtown Square, PA: Project Management Institute, Inc., 2013.

Project Management Institute. *The Standard for Risk Management in Portfolios, Programs, and Projects*. Project Management Institute, Inc., 2019.

Redmond-Jones, Beth. "Strengthening Our Core: How Defining Shared Values Can Revitalize Teams." American Alliance of Museums. Published June 25, 2021. https://www.aam-us.org/2021/06/25/strengthening-our-core-how-defining-shared-values-can-revitalize-teams/.

Redmond-Jones, Beth. *Welcoming Museum Visitors with Unapparent Disabilities*. Lanham, MD: Rowman & Littlefield, 2024.

Saich, Emily, and Joey Scott. "5 Ways to Keep Your Exhibit Project Moving…Remotely." *American Alliance of Museums*, May 15, 2020. https://www.aam-us.org/2020/05/15/5-ways-to-keep-your-exhibit-project-movingremotely/.

Saich, Emily, and Joey Scott. "REAL TALK: Assessing Feasibility with Collaborative Teams." *Exhibition: A Journal of Exhibition Theory & Practice for Museum Professionals* 40, no. 1 (Spring 2021): 40–47. https://static1.squarespace.com/static/58fa260a725e25c4f30020f3/t/626059188e780c45a3a15ea4/1650481432625/10_Exhibition_21SP_RealTalk.pdf.

Seiler, Rich. *The Pull Planning Playbook for Foreman and Superintendents: Learn the Coach's X's and O's to Pull Like Pros*. Unified Works, Inc., 2019.

Seiler, Tom. "Project Management." In *Manual of Museum Planning: Sustainable Space, Facilities, and Operations*. Third Edition, 541. Lanham, MD: AltaMira Press, 2012.

Serrell, Beverly. *Exhibit Labels: An Interpretive Approach*. 2nd ed. Rowman & Littlefield, 2015.

Serrell, Beverly. *Judging Exhibitions: A Framework for Assessing Excellence*. Left Coast Press, 2006.

Sigmond, Cathy. "The Many Shapes of Formative Evaluation in Exhibition Development." *Exhibition: A Journal of Exhibition Theory & Practice for Museum Professionals* 38, no. 1 (Spring 2019): 34–41. https://www.aam-us.org/wp-content/uploads/2024/04/09_Exhibition_TheManyShapesofFormativeEvalution.pdf.

Simon, Nina. *The Participatory Museum*. Museum 2.0, 2010.

Snelling, Rebecca. *Choosing by Advantages: How to Make Sound Decisions*. BDI Publishers, 2022.

Stoltz, Dorothy, Marisa Connor, and James Bradberry. *The Power of Play: Designing Early Learning Spaces*. Chicago: ALA Editions, an imprint of the American Library Association, 2015.

Sutherland, Jeff. *Scrum: The Art of Doing Twice the Work in Half the Time.* Crown Currency, 2014.

Tamm, James W., and Ronald J. Luyet. *Radical Collaboration: Five Essential Skills to Overcome Defensiveness and Build Successful Relationships.* 2nd ed. Harper Collins, 2019.

"The RFP Issue." *Exhibition: A Journal of Exhibition Theory & Practice for Museum Professionals* 26, no. 1 (Spring 2007). https://www.name-aam.org/exhibition_spring2007.

University of Washington Project Delivery Group. "Meet the 2021 Design-Build Project of the Year Team." Design-Build Delivers, December 2, 2021. https://designbuilddelivers.buzzsprout.com/2084451/11706950-meet-the-2021-design-build-project-of-the-year-team.

Whitemyer, David. "Practice Makes Perfect: 4 Keys to Exhibit Prototyping Success." *American Alliance of Museums*, June 29, 2018. https://www.aam-us.org/2018/06/29/practice-makes-perfect/?gad_source=1&gclid=CjwKCAjwqMO0BhA8EiwAFTLgINsqC6c8jxTbr44y77ONkDZfu4OplWJ1Ao24DwAqLgr7Du-leBKcPhoCMjAQAvD_BwE.

Witthoft, Scott and Stanford d.school. *This Is a Prototype? The Curious Craft of Exploring New Ideas.* Berkeley, CA: Ten Speed Press, 2022.

Woolley, Anita Williams, Christopher F. Chabris, Alex Pentland, Nada Hashmi, and Thomas W. Malone. "Evidence for a Collective Intelligence Factor in the Performance of Human Groups." *Science* 330, no. 6004 (October 29, 2010): 686–88. https://doi.org/10.1126/science.1193147.

Woolley, Anita Williams, Margaret E. Gerbasi, Christopher F. Chabris, Stephen M. Kosslyn, and J. Richard Hackman. "Bringing in the Experts: How Team Composition and Collaborative Planning Jointly Shape Analytic Effectiveness." *Small Group Research* 39, no. 3 (June 1, 2008): 352–71. https://doi.org/10.1177/1046496408317792.

Index

accessibility, 57, 58
accomplishments, keeping list of, 151
accountability, for deliverables, 9–10
action items, sharing, 45
Adamczyk, Joan: An Approach to Handling Project Changes, 137–38
adaptive challenges, 103–4
agenda setting, 43
alignment, 87; feasibility and, 93
appreciation: reflection and, 59; self, 151–52; team, 145–46
An Approach to Handling Project Changes (Adamczyk), 137–38
architect: meetings with, 131

bids, contractor, 129
boundaries, setting helpful, 152
brainstorming: blue-sky, 57–58; guidelines, 58
budget: approach to, 33; communication template, 35; conceptual, 34; construction contingency for changes to, 136; contingencies, 35–37, 36; cost to completion, 41n2; envelope, 17, 33–34; feasibility questions on, 94; final cost estimate for, 34; prototyping for, 79n11; report, 141–42; schematic estimate, 34, 35; team decisions on, 33; tracking, 34–35, 35; transparency, 35; variance sample, 35

calendar, changes recorded on, 132
celebrating, 145–47
challenges, problem-solving for, 103–4
changes: anticipating, 136; calendar noting, 132; change orders, 119–21, 120; handling project, 137–38; on-site, 135–38; personnel or team dynamic, 138; remediation report on, 142
charrettes, 58–60
clients: characteristics of best, 114; client-contractor relationship, 113–14
closeout phase, 6, 11
co-creation, 49–50, 54n4; activity for idea generation, 59
collaboration: co-creation in, 49–50, 54n4, 59; collaborators defined, 10; for holistic vision, 40; independence balanced with, 5, 50; process-making and, 10; schedule-making, 37–39, 38
collective feasibility, 93–95, 94
commissioning, 141
communication: connection prompts for, 146, 147; during construction, 131–34; with contractors, 112–13; difficult conversations and, 41; on-site, 131, 132; problem-solving with open, 106; template for budget, 35; transparency and, 40; visual, 62, 64

completion: accountability for deliverables and, 9; budget report and, 141–42; commissioning and, 141; cost from start to, 41n2; manuals and, 141; punchlisting, 139, *140*; remediation report, 142; retrospectives, 143–44; schedule report, 142

concept, *65*; deliverables, *8–9*; package, *11*; phase, *7*; prototyping, 74–75; rendering, *66*

concept sketch, *66*

conceptual budget, 34

conflict, productive and nonproductive, 87

connection: activities, 30; prompts, 146, *147*

consensus, 97

constraints, 16, 76–77

construction: communication during, 131–34; contingency, 36, 136; cost to completion, 41n2; daily site huddle, 131–32; design documentation for fabrication and, *65*; documentation, 6, 7, *8–9*; fabrication distinguished from, 6; installation and, 6, *7*, *65*, *94*; measure twice rule, 135–36; phase deliverables listed, *7–8*; punch listing midway through, 139, *140*; real-time drawing set, 132–33

construction site: changes on, 135–38; monitoring visitors of, 133; safety on, 133

consultants, 20

content developers, 22, 61, 151

content development, 11n4

contingencies: budget, 35–37; construction, 36, 136; design, 36; owner, 36–37

contractors, developing scope for, *119*; change orders and, 119–21, *120*; defining needs and, 115; sample scopes, 116–18

contractors, exhibit, 20, 109; asking authentic questions of, 127–28; asking questions of, 112, 129; awarding contracts to, 128–29; building trust with, 112–13; characteristics of best, 114; communicating with, 112–13; flexibility with, 113, 114; informing, 112; input and expertise of, 113; interviewing, 128; multiple prime, 125; not selected, 129; qualifications request (RFQ), 123–25; Request for Proposals, 125–26, 128; selecting, 123, 129; team-building as including, 112; types of, 111–12

contracts, awarding, 128–29

coordination models, 23, *23*, *24*

cost to completion, 41n2

creative development: design basis and, 55–56, 60; design documentation, 64–68, *65–68*; exhibit summaries, 62, *63*; idea generation, 49–52, 58–60; as beyond idea generation, 55; idea refinement stage, 60–62; independent work in, 61–62; interpretive approach and, 56; look and feel, 56; materials and maintenance, 57; vision, 47, 56; visual communication and, 62, 64

creativity: co-creation and, 49–50, 54n4, 59; creative openers, 50–52; facilitating, 49–53; sparking, 58

Crosby, Cortez: Embracing Challenges to Find Solutions, 106

curiosity, 150

daily site huddle, 131–32

decision-making: consensus, 97; delegation and, 98; divergent thinking and, 97; leadership team help in, 98; range voting for, *98*, 98–99; SWOT analysis for, 99, *100*

160　　　　　　　　　　　　　　　　　　　　　　　　　　　　　　　　　　　Index

delegation, in decision-making, 98
deliverables: accountability, 9–10; collaborators input and, 10; concept phase, 8–9, 65; definition of, 9; documentation of, 8–9, 8–9; in sample scope template, 116
design and design phase: basis of, 55–56, 60; contingency, 36; design-bid-build system, 125; design-build system, 125; documentation, 64–68, 65–68; drawings of final, 67; feedback, 64; final, 6, 7, 11n4, 65, 67; flexibility, 113–14; multimedia, 22
designers, exhibit, 151; multimedia, 22; visual communication for supporting, 64
design sprint (idea refinement strategy), 61
director role, 21
documentation, 5; budget report and, 141–42; closeout, 6; construction, 6, 7, 8–9; coordination models, 23, 23, 24; of deliverables, 8–9, 8–9; design, 64–68, 65–68; exhibit summaries, 62, 63; project brief, 17–18; prototyping, 76–78, 77; punch list and, 139, 140; real-time drawings and, 132–33; remediation report, 142; of roles and responsibilities, 26; schedule report, 142; unclear or missing information in plan, 137. *See also* project brief
drawings: concept sketch, 66; coordination model, 23, 23, 24; draw your neighbor exercise, 52; final design, 67; real-time site, 132–33

EBC. *See* Excite, Build, Consider
education representative, 22
elevation coordination drawing, 23
Embracing Challenges to Find Solutions, (Crosby), 106

empathy, 31, 37, 146, 150, 151
estimates, budget: final cost, 34; schematic, 34, *35*
Excite, Build, Consider (EBC) framework, 82–84, *83*
exhibit designer, 22, 64, 151
exhibit fabricator, 22
exhibition phases, *94*, 109; design documentation by phase, 65; framing feedback by, *84*, 84–85; list of, 6–7; overlapping nature of, 6–7; phase closeout, 6, *11*; planning, 65, 131; process overview, *7*; schedule report, 142. *See also specific phases*
exhibitions: celebrating work of, 145–47; director/head, 21; finding alignment for, 87, 93; sponsor, 33, 41n1; valuing diverse people involved in, 150–51. *See also specific topics*
exhibit summaries, 62, *63*

fabrication: construction distinguished from, 6; feasibility questions for, *94*; flexibility from design to, 113–14; phase, 6, 65; photo of final, *68*; scope sample for rockwork, 117–18; shop visits, 118–19, *119*
fabricators, 151
facilitation: creativity, 49–53, 54n4, 54nn1–2; definition of, 49; neutrality and, 50; for problem-solving, 104–5; reading the room, 52–53; for retrospectives, 143; setting for ideas and, 50
feasibility: alignment through understanding, 93; collective, 93–95, *94*; questions, 93, *94*; subjectivity and risk with, 95–96; when to assess, *94*
Feasible Fours, 61
feedback: from contractors, 113; design, 64; EBC framework for,

82–84, *83*; idea generation, 59–60; by phase, *84*, 84–85; product reviews for, 81–82
final design, 11n4; documentation, *65*; drawings, *67*; phase, 6, 7
flexibility, design to fabrication, 113–14
floor plan, marking, 135–36
Frameworks for Roles and Responsibilities (Ledesma), 26
From, Your General Contractor (Neidernhofer), 113–14
functional prototype, 75

general contractor, strong relationship between client and, 113–14
goals, 40–41, 47, 50, 53, 62; changes and, 138; charrettes and, 58–60; collective feasibility and, 93–95, *94*; designers and, 64; EBC, 82; idea refinement and creating, 60; looking to vision and, 106; product reviews and, 81; prototyping and, 74, 76, 78; schedule and, 37; sharing with contractor, 112; sustainability example, 57; unique, 127; visitor experience, 63
guest experience representative, 22

Hagen Tilp: The Motivation to Prototype, 76
humming and bumming, 89, *90*

idea generation, 49, 55; activities and recommendations, 58–60; creative openers for, 50–52; feedback and sharing in, 59–60
ideas: feasibility questions for, *94*; refinement of, 60–62; strategies for refining, 61–62; workgroup intensive, 62
immersion activity, 30

independence: collaboration balance with, 5, 50; making time for independent work, 61–62
information gathering, 119–21; information matrix template, *120*; before project brief, 13–15; unclear or missing information, 137
information sorting, from project brief, 15–17
infrastructure, 6, 151; feasibility questions on, *94*
insiders group, 31
installation phase, 6, 7, *65*; feasibility questions on, *94*
interpretive approach, 56
interviews, contractor, 128

Kelsey, Elin, 54n4
kickoff, project: connection activities for meeting, 30–32; hosting, 29–30
The "Kickoffs" before The Kickoff (Sakato), 30–32
Kim, Ed, 40–41; Working Side-by-Side with your Architect, 40–41

leadership: decision-making and team, 98; difficult conversations supported by, 41; team, 20, 98
Ledesma, Andrea, 11n5; Frameworks for Roles and Responsibilities, 26
living schedule, 132

manager, project, 27n3, 39, 40, 49–50, 137; lack of defining, 138; primary responsibility, 20–22, 33, 113
Manning, Jason, *66–68*
manuals, operations and maintenance, *65*, 141
markups, 132–33
materials, 140; feasibility questions for, *94*; testing, 75–76
materials and maintenance, 57; feasibility questions on, *94*

measurements: floor plan marking, 135–36; measure twice rule, 135–36; by multiple people, 135
meetings: agenda setting, 43; charrettes and, 58–60; daily site huddle, 131–32; notes, 44–46; one-on-one, 31–32; Owner, Architect, Contractor (OAC), 131; project kickoff, 30–32; sample scope template and, 117; show and tell, 132; status, 43–44; wall-to-wall, 44; working, 44. *See also* facilitation
Metcalfe Architecture & Design, 66–68
MOCHA framework, 26
The Motivation to Prototype (Tilp), 76–78
multiple prime contractors, 125

Neidernhofer, Shelley: From, Your General Contractor, 113–14
note-taking, 44–46

OAC. *See* Owner, Architect, Contractor
O&M manuals. *See* operations and maintenance
operations, 17
operations and maintenance (O&M) manuals, 65, 141
Owner, Architect, Contractor (OAC) meeting, 131
owner contingency, 36–37

Pair-Share, 59
paper clips, 52
paper prototype, 74
people, valuing products and, 150–51
phases. *See* exhibition phases
photo research services, sample scope for, 116–117
pilot product, 75
plan: floor, 135; prototyping, 72, 73; review, 137–38; unclear or missing information in, 137; work group, 39–40
planning phase, 65, 131
problem-solving: communication and, 106; embracing other perspectives in, 106; facilitation for, 104–5; finding solutions together, 104–5; identifying challenges before, 103–4; project vision and, 106; relationship-based, 104–5; technical vs. adaptive, 103–4; understanding challenges for, 104
processes: collaboration and independence encouraged by, 5; communicating, 11; flexible, 5; making own, 9, *9–10*; pace set by, 4; project size and, 10; tools and, 3–5
product reviews: for feedback, 81–82; in situ, 81
products: pilot, 75; valuing people and, 150–51
project: alignment, 87, 93; budget envelope, 17, 33–34; considerations, 16–17; constraints, 16; description, 15; goals, 16; kickoff, 29–32; location, 15; operational consequences, 17; purpose and rationale, 15–16; reporting stops in, 91, *91*; risks, 17; setting up, 1; size, 10; sponsor, 33, 41n1; stops and starts, 91, *91*; vision and goals, 106. *See also* exhibition phases; *specific topics*
project brief: definition, 13; documentation, 17–18; information gathering before, 13–15; inviting participants to, 14; materials and preparation, 14; meeting questions, 14–15; sections, 15–17; sorting information from, 15–17
project set-up, benefits of team collaboration on, 1

prototype: definition, 71; functional, 75; paper, 74; proof of concept, 74–75; team, 61

prototyping: budget and schedule, 79n11; documentation, 76–78, 77; feasibility questions for, 94; plan, 72, 73; prioritizing, 71–72; questions for analyzing outcomes of, 74; terminology, 74; testing and, 61; testing materials and safety, 75–76; when and what of, 72, 74–75

punchlisting, 139, 140

quality, 136–37

RACI framework, 26

range voting, 98, 98–99

rapport, building team: change inevitability and, 89; humming and bumming, 89, 90; starts and stops report, 91, 91

reading the room, 52–53

recognition, giving, 146–47

redlines, 132–33

refinement, idea, 60

reflection, appreciation and, 59

remediation report, 142

Request for Proposals (RFP), 125–26, 128; RFQ vs., 123

Request for Qualifications (RFQ), 123–25

resilience building, 150

retrospective review, project kickoff, 30

retrospectives, 143–44

review: plan, 137–38; product, 81–82; timing for remediation report and, 142

RFP. See Request for Proposals

RFQ. See Request for Qualifications

risks, project, 17; feasibility and, 95–96

rockwork fabricator, sample scope for, 117–18

roles and responsibilities: documenting, 26; frameworks for, 26; project team members, 19–20; role narratives, 20–22; scope directory for, 24, 25. See also manager, project; specific roles

safety: prioritizing construction site, 133; testing materials and, 75–76

Sakato, Tiffany: The "Kickoffs" before The Kickoff, 30–32

scenic rockwork fabricator, sample scope for, 117–18

schedule: buffer time and, 37; changes and, 120; changes to opening date, 136; charrettes and, 58; clearing, 60; collaboration in making, 37–39, 38; contractors and, 113; end date importance, 37, 38; feasibility questions for, 94; living, 132; project brief discussion of, 17; prototyping budget and, 79n11; report, 142; sample scope template and, 117; shop visits and, 119, 119; specialty fabrication in-person, 119; sticky note sample for, 38; as tool example, 3; updating, 4; work group plans and, 39–40

schematic estimate, 34, 35

schematic phase, 6, 7, 65, 67

scope, project, 16; change orders and, 119–21, 120; for contractors, 115–21; customizing for contractors, 115; definition, 115; directory, 24, 25; photo research services sample, 116–117; scenic rockwork fabricator sample, 117–18; for specific disciplines, 115

scope creep, 18n2

seating, 57

self-appreciation, 151–52

shared values, 90–91

shop visits, 118–19, 119

show and tell, 132

sponsor, project, 33, 41n1
squiggle bird, 51
status meetings, 43–44
sticky notes, 59; class photo, 52; for problem-solving discussions, 105; sample, for schedule-making, *38*
storyboards, 62
subcontractors, 111
subjectivity, feasibility and, 95–96
summaries, exhibit, 62, *63*
sustainability: materials consideration and, 57; resources, 69n7
SWOT analysis, 99, *100*

Tape it up, 51
team, project, 17; alignment with other teams, 87; appreciating, 145–46; budget and schedule decisions by, 33; changes in personnel or team dynamics, 138; collective feasibility, 93, 95; contractor interview and, 128; contractors as part of, 112, 114; core members, 31; extended, 20; feasibility questions for, 93, *94*; humming and bumming, 89, *90*; idea refinement, 60; members, 19–20; preparing for change, 89, *90*; process-building benefit for, 9; project kickoff involving entire, 29; project stops report and, 91, *91*; prototype, 61; recognition given to members of, 146–47; retrospectives, 143; role narratives, 20–22; shared values, *90*, 90–91; suggested members for tricycle refinement, 61; trust, 9; workgroup intensive, 62
technical problem, adaptive vs., 103–4
tech philosophy, 46

templates: budget communication, 35; deliverables scope, 116–17; meeting note, 45
Te Papa museum, 79n11
testing: materials and safety, 75–76; prototyping and, 61
themes and takeaways: building resilience, 150; embracing curiosity, 150; self-appreciation, 151–52; thinking big and small, 149–50; valuing people and products, 150–51
30 circles, 51
tools, 2
tools and processes: defining, 3; documentation, 5; as support system, 4
transparency, 35, 40
Tricycle refinement, 61
trust, 10, 105; with contractors, 112–13, 114

universal design (UD), 69n4

values, shared, *90*, 90–91
vendors, 112
vision, 47, 56; problem-solving and, 106
visitors: experience, 63; visitor services representative, 22
visual communication, 62, 64
voting, range, *98*, 98–99

Wall-to-Wall Wednesday, 44
Wild Fours, 58, 59, *59*
word association, 52
workgroup intensive, for idea refinement, 62
workgroup plans, 39–40
working meetings, 44
Working Side-by-Side with your Architect (Kim), 40–41

Index **165**

About the Authors

Emily Saich has over 20 years of experience in managing the planning, development, design, prototyping, and fabrication of exhibitions and innovative visitor experiences. She has worked on several award-winning and influential exhibitions and managed projects for all types of museums and organizations, including science centers, natural history museums, children's museums, public gardens, performing art centers, art museums, historic sites, zoos, and aquariums. Emily is director of Exhibition Projects at the Monterey Bay Aquarium, where she leads project strategy for major exhibitions and guides collaborative teams through design and creation of visitor-centered experiences. Emily has served on the board of the National Association for Museum Exhibitions and has experience teaching graduate-level museum studies at Johns Hopkins University. Emily holds a Bachelor of Arts in studio art from California Polytechnic University, Humboldt, and a Masters of Fine Arts from Tyler School of Art and Architecture at Temple University. And she is a practicing artist.

Joey Noelle Scott is manager of Exhibition Project Delivery at the Monterey Bay Aquarium, where she leads project teams that create innovative exhibitions to inspire conservation of the ocean. With 20 years of experience in educational and museum settings, she's led a diversity of projects, including the creation of curriculum, professional development programs, digital products, libraries, and exhibitions. She's built expertise in facilitation, program development, and project management, with a particular focus on developing processes that support collaboration and creativity. She has served on the board of the Southwest Marine Educators Association and as a reviewer for *Science and Children*, a publication of the National Science Teachers Association. Her formal training includes a Bachelor of Science in genetics, an MA in education, and a certification as a Project Management Professional and LEED AP ID+C.